EXTREME NZ

Clare Murphy

ABOUT THE AUTHOR In the course of research for this book, Alison Dench leapt from high places, threw herself into raging torrents, scaled impossible heights and descended at great speed. Rock climbing, though, remains her favourite pursuit – and she can be found at the crag indulging this personal obsession at every opportunity. When the need to earn a living interferes with her climbing, she writes, edits and designs a variety of books from her home office in Auckland.

First published in 2000 by New Holland Publishers (NZ) Ltd
Auckland • Sydney • London • Cape Town

218 Lake Road, Northcote, Auckland, New Zealand
14 Aquatic Drive, Frenchs Forest, NSW 2086, Australia
24 Nutford Place, London W1H 6DQ, United Kingdom
80 McKenzie Street, Cape Town 8001, South Africa

ISBN: 1 877246 36 0

Managing editor: Renée Lang
Cover design: Seven
Design: Seven
Editor: Sara Haddad

Front cover photograph: courtesy AJ Hackett Bungy
Colour reproduction by Colour Symphony Pte Ltd
Printed by Times Offset (M) Sdn Bhd

EXTREME NZ

A THRILLSEEKERS GUIDE

ALISON DENCH

ACKNOWLEDGEMENTS

The assistance and support of a number of people have not only made this book possible but made it a pleasure (some of the time) to write, and this is my chance to thank them. Renée Lang helped hatch this whole plot, had the confidence that I could do the job, and was encouraging and constructive throughout the production process. Barbara Nielsen supplied me with excellent ideas and good advice, and the occasional much-needed boot up the backside. Adventure tourism operators Julien Senamaud, Peter Chandler and Alan and Kirsty Hoffman were generous with their time and knowledge, Lee-anne Parore was an invaluable source of technical information, and Susan Ewen weighed in with professional guidance.

Thank you, also, to all the operators who hosted me on trips: without your support this book could not have been completed. And many thanks to Rob and Roz Greig, who gave me a room at their backpackers while I was doing my research. Here's that plug I promised:

Pinewood Lodge, 48 Hamilton Road, Queenstown

Freephone **0800 PINEWOOD (0800 746 396)** Website **www.pinewood.co.nz**

If once you've read and used this book you have ideas for how the book could be improved (or better still just want to tell me how much you've enjoyed it), if you've had a particularly good adventure tourism experience or a particularly bad one, or if you're an operator who'd like to be included in a future edition you can get in touch with me by email: ExtremeNZ@hotmail.com

CONTENTS

INTRODUCTION

Every country has its place on the world traveller's itinerary. At Pamplona you run with the bulls, at Chiang Mai you trek through the Karen villages, in Central Africa you bond with the gorillas. And in New Zealand you go bungy jumping, whitewater rafting and jetboating. There may be other places that specialise in this kind of thing – Interlaken, Victoria Falls – but New Zealand is surely the world's greatest adventure playground.

If there's one thing this country does really well, it's nature. It's everywhere and everywhere it's spectacular, from the volcanoes and subtropical forests of the North Island to the glaciers and crystal-clear mountain lakes of the South Island. And New Zealanders appreciate it. Every city dweller in this underpopulated country lives within a few hours of unblemished nature and most take advantage of it, whether it be hunting in the rugged hill country, fishing off the beautiful coastline or trekking in the the wilderness.

New Zealand has everything you need for extreme sports: mountains, raging rivers and warm, reasonably stable summer weather conditions. But most of all we have experience and a tradition of technical expertise and safety in the outdoors, as well as a reputation as innovators – an astonishing number of the adventure activities were either invented or first offered commercially here. There's a thrill for everyone: jetboating or hot air ballooning for the less active, river boarding or adventure caving for the fit, bungy jumping or skydiving for those looking for the big rush.

So what exactly are these "extreme sports" that get people so excited? In their purest form, extreme sports are sports invented originally for fun not competition, based in nature and with an element of physical (and perhaps psychological) danger that gives an adrenalin rush. And "adventure tourism"? The term covers a multitude of outdoor activities from the relatively tame – think horse riding – to such epic expeditions as scaling Mt Cook, all of them made available to tourists. It's the sports at the intersection of extreme sports and adventure tourism, the commercially operated outdoor activities that provide a thrill, that are the concern of this book.

But why? The question's inescapable. Why would you want to jump out of a plane, or risk your life on a whitewater river, or climb up a rock face? There are probably as many answers as there are part-time adventurers, and most people have a combination of reasons.

For some it's about rebellion. The media is peppered with advertising images of wild, live-fast-die-young extreme sports people clutching a soft drink or flashing a watch. We've been sold the idea that the beautiful people push the limits and that danger is cool; if we can overcome fear then we will find freedom.

For others extreme sports are a way of experiencing nature in a more visceral way. Swimming with dolphins or sharks, being tumbled and submerged by whitewater or soaring above the earth in a paraglider helps us to understand our true place in the world. In an age when technology is all around us, we offer ourselves up to nature's raw power.

Still others – those who try rock or ice climbing, say, or whitewater kayaking – want to do something new, to learn a new skill. For them it's important that if anyone's leading in this dance with nature it's them: the buzz comes from doing it themselves rather than entirely entrusting their safety to someone else.

Many tourists, however, don't really know what they're getting themselves into or why they're doing it – caving just sounds like a laugh or their mate back home went bungy jumping so they have to as well. For them adventure tourism offers an instant fix: you can go the same day you book and you save yourself the trouble of learning the necessary skills by leasing the time, experience, techniques and equipment of experts. For these people the pleasure may come less from the experience itself than from being able to tell the story afterwards. That's why it's so important to buy the T-shirt – it makes people ask you about it.

Whatever the reason people choose to try fully extreme activities like bungy jumping or skydiving, they all experience the same physical effects of stress. At the first sign of danger – and it doesn't matter if it's real or imagined – the body goes into "fight or flight" mode, a powerful response that gives a boost of energy and prepares the body to either confront the threat or escape it.

The hypothalamus, one of the most primitive parts of the brain, activates the pituitary gland, which releases into the blood a hormone that stimulates the adrenal glands to increase their output of adrenalin and cortisol. Muscles tense, the heart races, breathing becomes shallow and rapid, and feet and hands become cold. Sugar is released from the liver, the body's metabolic rate increases, digestion is inhibited and extra acid is secreted in the stomach. It's enough to make you sick, really.

The body is doing its best to preserve its owner, and part of the thrill of extreme sports comes from overcoming the natural instinct to avoid danger. In a heady cocktail, terror mingles with excitement: your body is telling you not to do it . . . but you're going to anyway.

And when, after the anxiety and anticipation of the build-up you choose fight over flight and actually do it – you run down the takeoff ramp or take the first tentative abseiling steps – the rewards come in an intoxicating rush. In a kind of corporeal meditation, thinking and feeling are reduced to the essentials: you are completely focused on survival. You feel fear, you may feel cold or heat, but you probably don't feel pain. You have an impression of speed, perhaps, and a new sensation of movement, and time speeds by and yet seems to stand still.

And then it's over. Your body quickly switches out of "fight or flight" mode and you can relax. But your mind is racing, reliving the experience, running through the what-ifs. You can afford to be pleased with yourself, even smug: you've done something most people would be too afraid to do, you've dominated both nature and your own body. The feeling of fear is replaced by elation and a sense of well-being that, sustained by a few celebratory drinks and extensive retelling of the tale, can last for quite some time. Your respect for nature has been deepened and you have a sense that you are special, that you have felt and seen things that ordinary people don't.

The thrill, though, doesn't always come from fear. In some activities – swimming with dolphins or seals and hot air ballooning, for example – it is more closely related to wonder and awe. Sometimes the rush comes from surviving the G forces and bodily battering of activities like aerobatic flights and Zorbing, and sometimes it results from meeting physical challenges, for example rock climbing, adventure caving and tackling a ropes course.

This whole extreme sports/adventure tourism thing began centuries ago when people started climbing mountains for no reason other than to see if it could be done. It wasn't until the late part of the 20th century that extreme sports really took off, in the form of skydiving, hang gliding, paragliding, bungy jumping and whitewater rafting.

Extreme sports and adventure tourism got going in New Zealand in the 1970s in Queenstown, when Shotover Jet started offering high-adrenalin jetboat trips, and soon after the whitewater rafting companies arrived. The alpine village got a reputation as a thrillseekers' heaven and before long operators were struggling to keep up with demand. At first most customers were New Zealanders, but this changed in the

1980s after AJ Hackett started the world's first full-time bungy operation on the Kawarau Bridge. Since then many dozens of adventure tourism operations have popped up in the the town, offering everything from hot air balloon flights to whitewater sledging, and Queenstown has bestowed upon itself the title of "Adventure tourism capital of the world".

By definition, adventure tourism involves some degree of risk. But extreme adventure doesn't have to mean extreme risk. Although the activities offered commercially in this country are inspired by dangerous extreme sports, they are more about personal challenge than risk-taking. In most cases there is very little chance of having an accident: the risk is perceived rather than real – although the fear is just as powerful.

You can't regulate the risk out of adventure entirely, but in an industry where good training, equipment, procedures and decision-making are a matter of life and death it is, fortunately, in the operators' long-term interests to minimise that risk. In the past some cowboy operators have sacrificed safety for short-term profit, but industry organisations have worked hard in recent years to change those attitudes.

People do die doing adventure tourism activities – but isn't that part of the thrill? In effect we're playing the odds, trusting that it's someone else's tragedy that's going to make this a "dangerous" sport. In any activity where we are at the whim of the elements accidents are a possibility, but in most the worst that's likely to happen is that you get a few bruises or a sprained ankle, maybe a cut. In fact, you're probably more likely to be killed driving a rental car or taking a scenic flight in a light plane or helicopter than doing adventure tourism.

It's easy sometimes to surrender responsibility for your safety to the experts, but don't forget that it's your responsibility too. As their own skill levels and confidence rise, guides may occasionally forget that it's not so easy for us, the punters. Their job is to push us as far as we can go, but we want to feel like we're taking risks – and *survive*. So look after yourself, use your common sense. If it feels wrong, turn back. Don't forget that fear can be a very useful emotion – sometimes it stops us doing really *stupid* things.

WHAT SHALL I DO?

As far as finding adventure thrills goes, different things work for different people. What terrifies me may be a walk in the park for you. Whitewater scares me but running off a hillside under a hang glider thousands of feet up barely raises my pulse. The opposite may be true for you – it really depends whether you're an air person or a water person. Some people, especially those who have done adventure activities before, have a very high tolerance for adrenalin, while others quail at the smallest threat (real or imagined) to their safety or are overwhelmed by challenge.

The activities described in the first part of this book are rated in two ways: adrenalin rush and personal input. In activities with a high adrenalin rating ■ ■ ■ □ **Adrenalin Rush** the thrill comes in a burst. In bungy jumping or tandem skydiving or bridge swinging, for example, it's that sinking feeling that gravity is dragging you to your doom, mitigated by faith that you will be saved at the last moment. Some of the activities with the highest ratings are over very quickly and bits – often the important bits – can be really quite unpleasant. But they do give the biggest and most intense rush, and make the best stories.

The lower the rating, the gentler the experience. For example in hot air ballooning, at the other end of the adrenalin spectrum, the thrill comes from a sense of awe and serenity, from having an experience of the landscape that not many are privileged to have. If you swim with dolphins or seals the thrill comes not so much in a rush of adrenalin as in a kind of nature ecstasy.

The thrill level may also depend on whether or not you're in charge. In activities with a low personal input rating ■□□□□ **Personal Input** you put your life in someone else's hands – jetboating and tandem paragliding are examples. If you're a control freak you may find this more stressful than doing things yourself. A high personal input rating means the activity requires a greater commitment to participation: you're the one making the decisions, choosing the line, making the moves.

Activities like whitewater sledging or boarding, canyoning, whitewater kayaking, rock and ice climbing, and doing a ropes course all require a high level of personal input. Although you're accompanied by a guide, you have to take responsibility for yourself. These skill-based activities are often the most rewarding; the thrill comes from taking on nature, and just getting through it is a personal triumph.

It's worth remembering that the experiences I had, as related in the first-hand accounts, are not necessarily representative of all operators in that category. The canyoning I did was low-key as canyoning goes, while my rafting trip was pretty extreme. In most activities there is a range of trips available to suit different temperaments.

WHERE SHALL I GO?

If you want to pack a lot of adventure into a short time – and have a fat wallet – you can't beat Queenstown, where there are dozens of operators waiting to give you the thrill of a lifetime. Don't imagine, though, that Queenstown is the only place you can do this kind of stuff: in the directory of operators you'll find companies that offer similar – or better – experiences all over the country.

The directory provides details of commercial operators that, on a regular or on-demand basis, offer activities providing an adrenalin rush for which no experience is necessary and all equipment is provided. To be included the activities had to be able to completed within one day and not require a group booking – although many operators also offer multi-day trips and can tailor-make trips for groups. They range from enthusiasts working out of the spare room to multinational organisations.

The listings are not paid advertising and so are as close to comprehensive as I can get them, but inevitably there are gaps: some operators did not respond to repeated approaches, some said they preferred not to be involved, and some that do not actively promote themselves may have escaped my notice altogether.

It is a directory, not a list of recommended operators, so an entry in it does not imply any kind of endorsement. The details given are as supplied and confirmed by the operators. In time the listings may become dated – prices change, ventures fail, new operators start up and old operators start offering new tours – but many adventure tourism outfits have been around a long time and will likely be around for a long time yet.

For most operators bookings are essential, although often a day's (or even a couple of hours') notice is enough. Occasionally, however, in the listings a street address is given: these operators may be able to look after you without a booking, although you may have to wait around a while. The prices quoted are for adults, but many operators offer discounts to groups, to travellers on particular bus tours, to YHA members and so on, and some have lower children's prices.

Enjoy the book – browse, surf, skim, and use it to help choose the right adventure for you. But remember this: testing the boundaries, taking risks and defying nature are not the be all and end all. Take a walk through the bush, go for a swim at a sandy beach, climb a hill and enjoy the view. They all have their own rewards, they don't require you to be frightened for your life – and best of all they're free.

AIR ADVENTURES

AEROBATIC FLIGHTS

Ratings	
■■■■□	Adrenalin Rush
□□□□□	Personal Input

Actionflite Aerobatics

On 25 September 1913 a crowd of 50,000 curious onlookers, including a fair smattering of rubber-neckers and ghouls expecting the worst, gathered at Brooklands aerodrome in Surrey, England. They were there to witness a daring attempt by pioneering French aviator Adolphe Pegoud to fly a monoplane upside-down. Having achieved an inverted flight of some hundreds of metres, a thrilling feat previously thought impossible, he flew a breathtaking sequence of loops, dives and rolls before returning gently to earth. The sport of aerobatics had been born.

Five years later, recently returned American World War I pilots flying used military aircraft began performing at "flying circuses" aerial stunts they had learned in combat – although many of them paid for their barnstorming with their lives. The US military started taking a real interest in aerobatics in the 1920s, with the Army Air Corps's aerial demonstration team – the Three Musketeers – taking to the skies in 1928.

These days civilian pilots all over the world are doing aerobatics for fun and competition, but New Zealand is one of only a very few countries where commercial passenger flights are permitted. Paying passengers aren't allowed in Europe or Asia, and it's not easily possible in the USA. Here, however, if you've got a commercial pilot's licence with an aerobatics rating and meet the Civil Aviation Authority's strict requirements you can take passengers up for the fastest adventure ride in New Zealand. There has never been an accident involving a commercial aerobatics plane in this country.

A number of operators with historic open-cockpit planes such as Tiger Moths offer romantic joyrides that include a few basic aerobatic manoeuvres, and in Wanaka for a mere $2000 you can take an aerobatic flight in a World War II P51-D Mustang. To get the ultimate stunt experience, though, you'll need to go to one of the operators that use the high-performance Pitts Special biplane. This purpose-built aerobatic plane is the sort you can see performing at airshows. Its power-to-weight ratio is extremely high and it is designed to withstand massive G forces.

G (gravity) forces are something you will need to know about – and will come to know about – if you take an aerobatic flight. Have you seen the videos of trainee astronauts whizzing around a centrifuge, their skin smeared all over their faces? They're experiencing positive Gs. When you're walking around normally you experience one unit of gravity or 1 G. Some manoeuvres in a stunt flight impose extra forces on your body that make you feel heavier than normal: at +4 Gs your body will feel as though it weighs four times as much as it normally does. Other manoeuvres will make you feel lighter than normal – these are negative Gs.

All these forces present a real challenge to the cardiovascular system, which battles to keep the body's extremities – including the brain – supplied with blood. This can lead to tunnel vision and eventually a blackout, although this should never happen on a commercial joyride. Because of the strain on the heart, if you've got a heart condition or are pregnant you must check with your doctor before taking an aerobatic flight. Impaired mobility may also be a problem, and if you are very large you may find it difficult to squeeze into the cockpit.

A lot of people are worried about motion sickness, but it's not really a big problem with aerobatics. If you don't get carsick or seasick, you shouldn't have any difficulty. And even if you do, don't let that stop you going up: the flights are short (usually 15–20 minutes) and you can always ask your pilot to back off the negative G manoeuvres – they're more likely to make you ill – if you start to feel sick during the flight.

Aerobatic flights are probably the least weather-dependent of the aerial adventures. Low cloud or high winds will halt flights, but that's about all. You don't need to bring anything special, just comfortable outdoor clothing. It's not a good idea to take a camera up with you: it's likely to end up flying around the cockpit, and looking through the viewfinder can be disorienting. Besides, most planes have a wing-mounted camera to take the pictures for you at a small extra cost. Prices for the flight itself start at around $150.

So, relax – if you can – and enjoy. You may never get another chance to see what an airshow stunt display looks like from inside the cockpit.

GETTING HIGH

There seems to be some kind of mistake. This can't be the *pilot* for my aerobatic flight. He is slim, tanned and good-looking – all the things you look for in a pilot – but he looks too young to be shaving, let alone flying a stunt plane. Brent reassures me that he *is* qualified and *does* have his aerobatics rating. Apparently he gets this all the time, the quizzing about how long he's been flying, when he got his licence. I am about to find out for myself just what he's capable of.

The first surprise is the plane. Actionflite's Pitts Special is tiny. There's only just enough room in it for pilot and passenger; the pilot sits at the back, ending up with his feet working the controls by the passenger's elbows.

But the real shock to the system is the take-off. We quickly build up speed on the grass airstrip, then we're off. Boy, are we off. I'm pushed deep into my seat (that's positive G force for you) by the thrust of the aircraft as we take off into the breeze at an angle Brent later judges to be 80°. Think about it. That's just 10° short of a completely vertical take-off.

I'm thoroughly unnerved by this astonishing lift-off and for the next five minutes, while we cruise towards Coronet Peak under a clear blue sky, my legs shake uncontrollably. I'm acutely aware of the large, rich lunch I've just eaten, and of the sick bag tucked strategically by my right hand.

The fun has only just begun. Brent tells me through my headphones that we've reached 4000 feet above the ground and it's time to get going with the stunts. He'll start gently with a loop. It's not all that gentle, it seems to me, as the positive Gs take effect and the horizon disappears before the negative Gs kick in and the ground reappears above my head. My knuckles are white, but so far so good.

Next it's a stall turn, Brent informs me. We fly directly up for a while before yawing gently, floating deliciously in mid-air, then tumbling into a directly downward flight. I've never experienced anything like this before. Although I'm being very firmly held by a five-point harness plus a lap belt, I feel the need to grasp the underside of the dash tightly as my body and mind are thrown into turmoil by the barrage of unfamiliar stimuli.

After this it all becomes a blur, and I'm not really sure if I'm enjoying it or not. The plane can rotate around three axes, and sometimes we're rotating around all three at once. Overwhelmed by the spinning, rolling images, I close my eyes, but I quickly realise that I'm missing out on half the experience. I reach a compromise with my instincts – thereafter when I'm feeling wobbly I close only one eye.

This is a full-on assault on the body and the senses, and occasionally I feel dizzy – I even start to get tunnel vision. Once or twice, when it all gets too much, I give Brent the thumbs-down, a prearranged signal that I need a break. Each time, after a few seconds' level flight I'm ready for more and I give him the thumbs up.

After six or seven minutes of stunts we're returning to the airport and I'm half disappointed and half relieved. Back on the ground I sit down with Brent and we go over the manoeuvres he's taken me through. In all the confusion of earth, sky and horizon I have gained absolutely no sense of what we've just done – barrel rolls, aileron rolls, 10 seconds of flying upside down, Cuban eights, reverse Cuban eights, stall turns with vertical rolls, a lomchivak, a slow roll and a hesitation roll. As he uses his cellphone as a model plane to illustrate I finally get some concept of what I've experienced.

As it turns out, it isn't even a particularly extreme routine, pulling only -1 to +4.5 Gs. I discover Brent thought I was feeling nauseous when I gave him the thumbs-down and took it easy on the negative G manoeuvres, the ones that make you float out of your seat.

Still, it's enough for me. It is a quite extraordinary experience, unlike any I've ever had, an altogether *other* experience. Always, perversely, I felt completely safe. And I didn't need the sick bag.

→   Actionflite Aerobatics, Queenstown.
Freephone 0800 360 264.

TANDEM HANG GLIDING

In the 1970s, the early days of the hang gliding craze, the sport earned a reputation for being seriously dangerous. Crashes were common and many pilots died. There were a number of reasons for this: the hang gliders were almost all home-built, the early technology was hit-or-miss, and the pilots tended to be self-taught.

Things have changed, thank God. The technology has developed and glider design has been constantly refined over the years. Hang gliders are now much easier to control and no longer disintegrate when you look at them the wrong way (in fact gear failure is incredibly rare), and good pilot training programmes are in place. There's a bumper sticker doing the rounds that says "Remember when sex was safe and hang gliding was dangerous?" It makes a fair point.

So what exactly is a hang glider? It's an unpowered aircraft in which the pilot, suspended beneath a single fabric wing, controls the flight by shifting his or her body weight. Hang gliders are usually launched from a high place, although sometimes they are towed aloft, and they rely on lift from thermals to sustain flight. A German called Otto Lilienthal is credited with inventing the hang glider in the 1890s, but modern hang gliders were not invented until 1963 when Australian John Dickenson developed NASA scientist Francis Rogallo's early ideas into the sort of hang glider we would recognise today. It was not until the 1970s that the recreational use of hang gliders really, well, took off.

Tandem hang gliders, in which a passenger can be suspended alongside the pilot, are a more recent innovation. Sky Trek began New Zealand's first commercial tandem flights in Queenstown in 1992 and for a long time they were the only operators, but in the last few years other companies have started offering tandem flights both in Queenstown and in Nelson.

Hang gliding pilots claim that their form of flying is the purest, and they're probably right. A hang glider, with a maximum speed of around 60 kph, flies faster than a paraglider and its glide ratio (the rate at which it loses altitude compared to distance covered) puts paragliders in the shade. It performs more like a soaring bird than any other aircraft and the method of control – weight-shift – is the simplest and most instinctive. Even the prone flight position is more natural and bird-like than, say, sitting in the seat of a paraglider or the cockpit of a glider.

Hang gliders, like gliders and paragliders, use rising air to gain altitude, and under the right conditions flights can be sustained almost indefinitely: hang glider pilots have travelled 500 km in a single flight, and thermalled their way up as high as 20,000 feet. Tandem flights, however, generally last 10–20 minutes, which is quite long enough to get a good taste of soaring flight. You can expect to pay $130–$145 per flight, depending on where you go.

This sport is weather-dependent. Rain, too much or too little wind, gusty wind or wind from the wrong direction can all cause cancellation, so it's a good idea to plan your flight for the beginning of your stay. For ideal conditions wait for a day with lightish winds and puffy clouds; afternoons are often better than mornings because there is more rising air off ridges. Because of the reliance on the weather, when conditions are right most operators will continue flights as long as there is daylight.

Hang gliding's a very photogenic sport, and operators usually offer in-flight photos at extra cost. Some use fixed cameras mounted on the wing and some have moveable cameras that can get shots from different angles, including front-on. This second option tends to give better, more varied results; usually they take a roll of 12 photos.

Most companies won't take children younger than 10, but there is no maximum age. There is a maximum weight, however: to fly safely the passenger needs to weigh 100 kg or less. You don't need to be fit, although generally you'll need to be able to run reasonably fast for 20 metres or so. If the head wind is strong enough, however, the running isn't necessary and people with restricted mobility can fly.

Commercial tandem flights have an excellent safety record in this country: in tens of thousands of flights there have been no fatalities or serious injuries. This is partly because tandem gliders are designed to be stable and partly because the pilots are trained thoroughly and are regulated by the New Zealand Hang Gliding and Paragliding Association. A number of New Zealand's tandem pilots are current or past national or world hang gliding champions.

Questions to ask

1. Do you have take-off sites to suit all wind directions?
2. Are customers taken to the take-off site in groups or as individuals? (If you're in a group you'll have to wait longer.)
3. Does the flight have a time limit, or will you continue flying as long as conditions allow?
4. If you offer action photos, are they taken by a static wing camera or a moveable camera?

FLY LIKE AN EAGLE (EAGLE, EAGLE)...

My pilot John is world speed gliding champion. That means he specialises in going very close to the ground very fast. I gulp. He promises not to scare me too much. I don't know if I believe him: his smile is just a touch too goofy and his shirt a touch too Hawaiian.

We're by the side of the road just below the Coronet Peak ski field, 2200 feet above the Wakatipu Basin. John has taken the rolled-up glider off the roof of the four-wheel-drive and is putting it together. I decide not to talk to him while he's doing it – I'd really hate to distract him. A few minutes later, when he's finished and I've had a good chance to get anxious, I put on a helmet and climb into the padded full-length harness. John talks me through the take-off routine, then walks me through it without the glider. He pats a pouch on the front of his harness. "The parachute," he says. I give a wan smile: I don't find this particularly reassuring.

Next thing I know I'm standing under the glider with one arm round his shoulder and the other holding the bottom of the harness out of the way, waiting for a gust of wind. When he says "Go!" we take a couple of steps down the short, mown grass strip, then break into a fast run. Suddenly I'm running in thin air like Wile E. Coyote. By the time I've worked my feet into the single stirrup attached to the harness the ground has disappeared and we're soaring.

I lie in comfort on my stomach and take things in while John beside me controls the hang glider using the triangular frame in front of us. The quiet is startling; to be flying without the drone of an engine is new to me and I *like* it. The wind on my face makes me feel utterly alive. There's a real sense of speed: the wind is whistling past us and we're covering a lot of ground. At times the tops of the pine trees seem very close. John reckons we're hundreds of feet above them but we're low enough to scatter the wild goats on the hillside.

We cruise gracefully along the ridge line looking for lifting air to extend the flight. I make believe I'm an eagle soaring lazily in the crisp morning, wings wide, taking advantage of any rising air I find. It's not hard to imagine: this has to be the closest a human being can come to flying like a bird.

John jolts me out of my reverie by throwing in a couple of tight, pitching turns to keep me honest – and to get a good photo. He gives me the opportunity to take control of the hang glider. In a half-hearted way I take the bar as instructed and try to steer but, to tell the truth, I'm quite happy to hand back control to the expert and just enjoy the ride.

We seem to be descending rapidly now and I'm crestfallen when John points out where we're going to land. But first there's the aerobatics: John, it seems, specialises in stunts. He suddenly throws his body forward and we pitch violently down until we're vertical or even past vertical, then roll out back into level flight. The sudden change of speed and direction is disorienting and disturbing, even frightening. We're bloody close to the ground now, but John throws in another wingover to truly terrify me.

Then suddenly it's all over as we sweep in for a silky smooth landing. I can't think of 10 minutes of my life that have passed quicker.

→ Antigravity Hang Gliding, Queenstown.
   Freephone 0800 HANG GLIDE (0800 426 445).

TANDEM PARAGLIDING

Ratings	
■■☐☐☐	Adrenalin Rush
■☐☐☐☐	Personal Input

Queenstown Tandem Parapentes

First things first. Don't ever insult a paragliding fanatic by suggesting that a paraglider is the same thing as a parachute. A paraglider is similar to a modern, steerable parachute but it is not identical. They may look alike, but parachutes are designed mainly to descend whereas paragliders are designed mainly to soar.

The history of the sport of paragliding is fairly hazy, and it's intertwined with the history of both skydiving and hang gliding. It's generally agreed that Americans Francis and Gertrude Rogallo came up with the early designs for "a flying machine with no rigid element or element designed to produce rigidity" in the 1940s, but it wasn't until the 1980s that paragliding became established as a sport after climbers in the French Alps started to use skydiving canopies to descend from peaks after completing technical routes. Now it's enormously popular world-wide and getting more so every day.

Like hang gliders, paragliders are launched by either running off a high place or by being towed up. They can get lift from warm air coming off the ground or breezes sweeping up off ridges. They're able to soar because the wing (the equivalent of the parachute's canopy) is held in shape by air pressure on the leading edge, inflating cells within the wing. Much like modern parachutes they're steered using two toggles that each pull down one corner of the banana-shaped wing. Paragliders, with a maximum speed of around 40 kph, are slower than hang gliders but they are lighter and more portable, and easier to learn how to fly.

Queenstown is undoubtedly the home of paragliding in New Zealand: the sport got a foothold there in the mid-1980s, when paragliding was still a novelty. On a good-weather day tandem parapentes – they call them by their French name in Queenstown – stream off Bobs Peak from the Skyline complex, one every couple of minutes or so. It doesn't stop there, though: there are now commercial tandem paragliding operations all over the country.

Paragliding is regulated by the New Zealand Hang Gliding and Paragliding Association, which assesses pilots for a special tandem rating that allows them to take passengers. Most commercial tandem flights last 10–20 minutes and cost between $100 and $130, but some companies also offer heli-tandems and longer flights. Another alternative is to do an instructional course: for $150–$160, not much more than the cost of a 15-minute tandem flight, you could be flying solo after just a day.

Most tandem paragliders are happy to take children and older people up. Some are able to take people with restricted mobility, but others require you to be able to run for the take-off. If you have any other major medical conditions you should tell the pilot, but that probably won't rule you out of taking the flight. Passengers usually need to weigh no more than about 100 kg, but if you're heavier than that it's worth checking with the operator because some pilots are able to take people up to 130 kg or even 150 kg.

Paragliding is highly weather dependent, so don't leave it till the last minute. Rain's no good, and winds have to be light and coming from the right direction. Spring and summer are generally pretty good times to go, although most operators fly year-round. Whenever you take your flight, remember to bring warm outdoor clothing with you: it gets chilly up there, even in summer.

It has to be said that this sport as a whole doesn't have the best safety record in the world, but commercial tandem pilots in this country are qualified, experienced and know the local conditions well – and for them accidents are so rare that the risk is almost negligible.

Questions to ask

1. Do you have take-off sites to suit all wind directions?
2. Are customers taken in groups or as individuals? (If you're in a group you'll have to wait longer.)
3. Does the flight have a time limit, or will you continue flying as long as conditions allow?

FLYING WITHOUT WINGS

On a crisp, clear, almost too-perfect morning I trudge up the hill at the top of the gondola behind my pilot, Bill, from Queenstown Tandem Parapentes. He's acting as his own sherpa, toting the enormous backpack that holds his paraglider. Not surprisingly he's puffing by the time we get to the take-off point 2000 feet above Queenstown.

I put on a bike helmet, jump into my clunky harness and waddle clumsily around while Bill prepares the bright-yellow paraglider on the ground and briefs me with a smoothness of delivery that hints at the thousands of times he's given this speech before. Once he's satisfied that everything's in order with both me and the wing, he buckles me to the front of his harness, which is in turn linked to the paraglider.

We face into the wind, looking down a gently sloping grass ramp worn smooth by myriad paragliders' feet. We wait for a gust of wind on our faces to help inflate the wing, then step firmly down the hill – and feel the wing take off, catch the breeze and try to pull us back. We strain forward, fighting the wing, until finally we get some momentum and we're sprinting down the hill.

Within seconds we're off the ground and going up. This comes as something of a surprise to me. To my inexpert eye a paraglider looks pretty much like a parachute, and I certainly wouldn't expect a parachute to go *up*. But we're not sinking gracefully: we're flying.

And an extraordinary sort of flying it is. It feels to me like a cross between flying and floating. Two thousand feet up there's no real sense of distance covered but I can tell we're travelling at speed because my hands are cold and my eyes are watering. There is no sound but the wind.

I relax into the comfortable, padded sit-harness – it's almost as good as an armchair – and marvel at the Queenstown panorama. It's 9.30 am but below us the lie-abed town is still quiet, with only the occasional ant traversing the sidewalks. The dense blue lake, mountains rising steeply from its shores, stretches away from us. I feel absolutely no fear. I belong up here.

For a good five minutes we spiral gently up and down above our take-off point, taking advantage of a thermal created by the morning sun hitting the grass ramp. We could go on like this indefinitely – and I would be quite happy if we did – but it's time to start the descent and we make a slow, sweeping turn away from the hill and out over downtown Queenstown and the wharf.

We soar over the town for a while, gradually losing height as we float, swoop and roll into turns. From time to time Bill whips out his camera-on-a-stick to take a photo of the pair of us. With my eyes and nose streaming from the cold wind, I'm not at my most glamorous, but there's no need for him to ask me to smile for the camera because I've got a permanent grin.

Bill throws in a couple of steeply spiralling spins. It's enough to make me dizzy and, as my stomach is propelled towards my feet by the G forces, glad I didn't have breakfast before the flight. The manoeuvres mean we lose height rapidly and soon we're nearing our landing site, a school playing field not far from the bottom of the gondola.

We neatly avoid the rugby goalposts and the passers-by using the field as a shortcut to Pinewood Lodge, and make a smooth, confident, stand-up landing. *Very* nice. And Bill is the one who has to make the walk up the hill to the gondola with the wing on his back, not me.

→ Queenstown Tandem Parapentes.
Freephone 0800 4 PARAGLIDE (0800 472 724).

Skydive Tandem (The Ultimate Jump)

TANDEM SKYDIVING

Ratings

■■■■■ Adrenalin Rush
□□□□□ Personal Input

Skydiving would have to be the ultimate thrill. How could you get more of a rush than by hurtling towards the ground at terminal velocity for half a minute or more? For many, many people (including me) skydiving is a long-held ambition, something they just have to try. And once is usually enough.

It used to be that before you could do a freefall jump you had to undergo days of theoretical and practical training, and do several static-line jumps. Since the mid-1980s, however, with the development of tandem parachutes, rank beginners have been able to experience freefall with only about 10 minutes' training. With an experienced tandem master literally on your back, you don't have to worry about anything except wetting your pants.

The story of the invention of the parachute is a long and blood-splattered one. For thousands of years people have been leaping off towers with various bizarre air-catching devices in the vain hope that they would float gently back to earth. In the 15th century Leonardo da Vinci came up with the first sensible design for a parachute, although another 300 years passed before in 1797 Frenchman André-Jacques Garnerin made the first successful jump. He used a silk parachute stiffened by rods – although all the way down he oscillated wildly as the air spilled first from one side of the unvented canopy then the other.

Parachutes were for the next century or so used for exhibitions, but in World War I they came into their own as an escape route from doomed observation balloons. In 1919 American Leslie Irvin made the first intentional freefall jump and the modern sport of skydiving was born. Since that time parachutes have been continuously refined and developed, to the point that the modern parachute, with its ram-air canopy, is a steerable flying machine rather than a simple descent device.

Tandem parachutes have extra-large canopies because of the extra weight being carried. The tandem master carries both a main chute and a reserve chute on his (yes, they're usually men) back. There is also a very small "drogue chute" that works during freefall to stabilise the skydivers and slow their descent slightly. The passenger's harness is clipped tightly to the front of the tandem master's harness.

Even with the drogue chute you'll achieve a terminal velocity of around 190 kph. It takes around 11 or 12 seconds and 1500 feet to reach terminal velocity and after that you drop 1000 feet every 6 seconds or so. In this country a lot of tandem jumps are from 9000 feet, which gives about 30 seconds of freefall before the chute opens at 4000 feet. At this height jumps cost between $145 and $245 – a very wide range in price when you consider that really the only important difference between operations is the view you get from the air. Pay a bit more, and you can jump from 12,000 feet, which gives you about 50 seconds of freefall. The 4000-foot float under the canopy takes about 5 minutes.

You don't have to be fit or strong to do a tandem jump, and there is no maximum age for passengers. Some operators will take children as young as four or five, although you have to wonder whether that's a good idea. You must tell the operator if you have any serious medical conditions but there are very few that would rule you out – some operators have taken people with major disabilities. If you weigh more than 100 kg I'm afraid you'll be too heavy to jump.

Weather conditions have to be good and the jump will be cancelled if there is wind, rain or low cloud. Summer and autumn are generally agreed to offer the most reliable conditions, although a winter jump in a mountainous region is spectacular. Year-round it's going to be damn cold up there at 9000 feet or more, so wear warm, comfortable, loose clothing and sensible, flat shoes.

Most of New Zealand's many operators can supply photos of you taken by a camera on the wing just before you exit the plane, but many also offer air-to-air photos and/or video taken by an aerial photographer who jumps with you. Needless to say this costs more, and you will need to book ahead.

And now to the sticky subject of safety. There can be no beating about the bush on this subject: both in New Zealand and overseas skydivers have been killed doing tandem jumps, usually because of gear failure. However, the odds of your twisting your ankle on landing, let alone being killed, are very, very long – many New Zealand tandem operators claim a 100 percent safety record over tens of thousands of jumps. Tandem masters, who in this country are required to have the New Zealand Parachute Federation's tandem rating, are amongst the most skilled and experienced skydivers there are; they simply do not risk the kind of dangerous manoeuvres that have been blamed for many skydiving deaths.

So rest assured that tandem skydiving isn't as dangerous as most people think – but you don't have to tell them that when you're boasting about your jump!

Questions to ask

1. Can I jump from a higher altitude for an extra cost?
2. Do you offer air-to-air photos and video?
3. How long will I have to wait before going up?

GOD'S OWN DROPZONE

As I pull on an ugly jumpsuit, absurd goggles and nerdy soft helmet I realise that skydiving is not a glamour sport. No that's not true – it's just not glamorous for tandem bunnies like me who get all the old-fashioned gear. I step into the harness and tandem master Matt adjusts the buckles. He runs through the procedure: how to position ourselves at the door, how to leave the plane and how to get into the best arched freefall position: think one, two, three, banana!

I find it hard to concentrate, though, because all I can think about is how loose the harness feels. I don't like to say anything – Matt surely knows what he's doing – but then I don't want to fall out of the harness at 10,000 feet either. After a long internal dialogue I decide to say something. Matt laughs. He reassures me that he'll tighten it later. He just didn't want me to be uncomfortable while we waited. Well, don't I feel dumb.

Minutes later eight of us are crammed like sardines into the plane as it trundles along the runway and makes heavy work of the take-off. And so begins the interminable spiralling flight up. I sit in front of Matt, jammed between his legs. The butterflies in my stomach are getting bigger – they're more like huge, mutant, tropical moths now. My knuckles are white and my fingernails are quarrying into my palms. I'm beginning to understand what I've got myself into, and I start running through the what-ifs. What if both chutes fail? Worse, what if I humiliate myself completely by refusing to jump?

Eventually the pilot gives the nod and someone opens the plastic blind that serves as the door. A rush of icy air is the first reminder that this is for real – we're 10,000 feet up. People start disappearing, including my friend Maria, whose stupid idea this was in the first place. Then, strangely, as Matt pulls the harness so tight that I'm pressed hard against his body I suddenly lose my fears. We're in it together. We bum-shuffle to the door and I put my feet outside and inch further out. Now there is simply no possibility of failing to jump.

I force out a smile and a wave for the wing camera, then cross my arms across my chest. Matt counts down . . . three . . . two . . . and we're out of the plane, tumbling through the slip-stream then plunging head-first towards the ground. It's disorienting and, for a moment, absolutely terrifying. This is much more brutal than I expected. I begin the count – one, two, three – the drogue chute slows us down – then Matt taps me on the shoulder and I arch my back and spread my arms.

At last we're stable. I relax a bit and try to make the most of the experience. I'm surprised to find there's really no sense of falling: at this height the ground doesn't appear to be getting any closer. There is just a sense of immense speed as cold, cold air blasts my face and the wind roars past my ears and tries to suck my goggles off. I drag my eyes away from the ground directly below me – it is quite mesmerising – to look around. It's quite a view but it's hard to take it in.

I reach a state of total acceptance. This situation is beyond my control. If the chute opens it opens, if it doesn't I'm dead: *que sera sera*. But the freefall goes on, and on, and the ground gets closer, and panic starts to overlay the ambivalence. Then there's a jolt as the main chute is released. I wait a second or two to allow it to open fully – I don't want to scare myself – then look up to check the canopy's OK. It is. Relief washes over me. I'm safe.

I can now afford to enjoy the experience. I savour the sense of floating/flying and relish the bird's-eye view of green fields, golden sand dunes and white surf breaking on the beach. I try to spot my friend Maria but can't see her. Matt points her out: she's well below us. "Don't worry," he says, "we'll catch her up." He pulls down hard on one steering toggle and we start a rapid, spiralling descent but after just a few seconds the spinning sensation makes me feel queasy. I have to ask him to stop before we've made it to waving-distance of Maria.

The five-minute float seems oddly shorter than the 35-second freefall and before I've had time to get used to the change of pace the ground is coming towards us very fast and Matt is turning into the wind to make the landing. I raise my knees at the last moment and Matt brings us in for a textbook touchdown. After he unbuckles me from his harness he shakes my hand and gives me a gentlemanly kiss. I hug him, and hug him hard. This man just saved my life.

In the car on the way home silence reigns. The experience has achieved something quite rare: it has left me lost for words.

HOT AIR BALLOONING

Ratings	
■□□□□	Adrenalin Rush
■□□□□	Personal Input

It's not clear which of the passengers of the first hot air balloon flight was the pilot – the sheep, the duck or the rooster – or even what their names were. The Montgolfier brothers, of course, accepted the plaudits for the flight at Versailles, France, in September 1783. They also took the credit for the first free flight made by humans two months later – although the fact they elected to send up a couple of associates instead of making the flight themselves suggests they may not have had complete confidence in their design.

Nonetheless, they sparked an interest in lighter-than-air flight that has, via an occasionally explosive detour into hydrogen-filled balloons, resulted in the high-tech recreational balloons we know today. Modern balloons are rather safer and more stable than the Montgolfiers' paper or fabric balloons: they're usually made of super-light rip-stop nylon with, reassuringly, a highly fire-resistant material used in the lower portions close to the propane burners that heat the air.

There's no doubt about it, hot air ballooning is at the "soft" end of the adventure tourism market. It's the least demanding of the air adventure sports and it's not going to make adrenalin course through your body – unless you suffer from vertigo – but it does give a thrill of another sort. There's something very romantic about hot air balloons; the idea of escaping gravity's bonds, of floating, unhurried, thousands of feet above mere earthlings, is an intensely alluring one. There may not be much to do except look at the view, but what feelings of freedom that bird's-eye perspective inspires!

New Zealand has a number of commercial balloon operators all offering a fairly similar service. Pilots have to have a Civil Aviation Authority licence and there is generally space for six to eight passengers. Children as young as five or six are usually welcome – although they may not necessarily be able to see all that much over the edge of the basket. Passengers don't need to be fit, but impaired mobility is likely to be a problem as you will have to stand for an hour to an hour and a half.

Almost all flights are made at dawn to take advantage of light winds and to make the most of the magic of sunrise. Ballooning is completely weather-dependent: rain, high winds or wind from the wrong direction will all cause cancellation, so if you are travelling it pays not to leave your flight till the end of your stay. (One passenger on the flight I took had made five attempts to take a balloon flight in various countries, all cancelled.) Autumn and winter are most likely to provide ideal conditions for ballooning because it's less often windy then. Winter is particularly good in areas close to mountains – for example, Taupo, Queenstown and Methven – because then the peaks will be capped with snow. You'll need to take warm clothes whatever time of year you go.

Ballooning is an expensive sport. The balloons themselves are very costly and have a limited lifespan, and the extreme dependence on the weather means that lots of flights have to be cancelled. The result is that ballooning comes in at the luxury end of the adventure tourism market, with one-hour flights costing anything from $200 to $300, although nearly always you'll find that included in the price is a champagne (or at least sparkling wine) breakfast once you touch down. For most people it's a once-in-a-lifetime experience worth every penny.

One final word: hot air ballooning may give the impression of being a perfectly gentle, safe and secure activity but this is deceptive. You should be aware that around the world many people have died in commercial ballooning accidents, although to be fair the actual number of accidents is relatively low. It's just that on the extremely rare occasion that things go wrong – the balloon being carried out of control by the wind, or hitting power lines – they go badly wrong for everyone on board.

Questions to ask

1. How many people will there be in the balloon?
2. Will there be spare clothing if I haven't got enough to keep me warm?
3. What do you supply in the way of food and drink after the flight?
4. Are cheaper stand-by fares available?

ASCENT INTO HEAVEN

The call from Queenstown's Sunrise Balloons comes at 6 am. The flight's on. I don't know if I'm pleased or disappointed – at this hour I could quite happily go back to sleep. When the taxi driver arrives, however, he tells me I should count myself lucky I'm not taking the flight in December or January, when the wake-up call comes at 5 am. A full moon watches over us on the drive to the take-off point and wisps of mist cling to the tarns. It's going to be a beautiful day.

Our first task when we arrive is to help inflate the balloon. While the burners blaze in the murky pre-dawn we help hold open the mouth of the balloon, which is stretched limply on the ground. It doesn't take long and soon the rainbow-striped balloon is upright and we are hauling ourselves into the wicker basket.

Hugh, our pilot, sets the noisy gas burners going and we're lifting gently away from earth. The rate of ascent takes me by surprise: within minutes we're 2000 feet above the ground. There's no sense of great height, rather of the ground gradually becoming more distant. Tethered only to the breeze, we drift softly over deer farms, vineyards, mobs of sheep. They seem too distant, almost unreal. The rays of the rising sun touch the mountain tops with a golden glow while misty cloud lingers in the valleys below. The views are magnificent and I click off some photos. But I realise they can never do the impossibly large landscape justice and after a while I put the camera down and simply breathe in my surroundings.

We ascend to 5400 feet above sea level. We are higher than the mountains that flank the Wakatipu Basin and can see further now, to the higher mountains beyond, snow-capped even in summer. The low angle of the sun accentuates the contours of the glacial moraine below us, while the vista of two arms of the huge lake, one stretching south, the other west, is quite stunning.

With a tug on a line Hugh keeps the balloon rotating so that all of us, trapped in our two-person compartments, get to enjoy 360° of magical scenery. I'm wearing five layers of clothing but I'm feeling chilly, so in spite of the noise I'm glad when from time to time Hugh fires the burners to regain height – the warmth on the back of my neck is very pleasing. But I'm also glad when the burners stop and the serene silence returns.

As we float high above the sleeping world there's such a feeling of isolation and timelessness that it comes as a shock when Hugh starts talking about landing. It's hard to believe an hour has passed. During our gradual descent we hover for a while over Lake Hayes and I have my first and only pang of anxiety during the flight as I consider the possibility of a water landing. It's a silly worry, I know, but I'm relieved when we clear it.

Hugh has permission to land from almost all the farmers in the basin, so he can pick and choose where we touch down. He selects a gently rolling field far from the road and as the ground seems to rush at us we brace for a hard landing – but it's surprisingly gentle and we don't tip over as I feared we might.

A few minutes later Hugh's family arrive in a four-wheel-drive and while they set up for breakfast we help Hugh pack up the balloon. We toast our successful flight with champagne and nibble on a breakfast of filled croissants and home-grown fruit.

For all of us a dream has just come true.

→ Sunrise Balloons, Queenstown.
  Freephone 0800 HOT AIR (0800 468 247).

FLY BY WIRE

Ratings	
■■■■☐	Adrenalin Rush
■■■■☐	Personal Input

Fly by Wire

The idea came to New Zealander Neil Harrap in the middle of the night: a giant swing that you could control by steering it, a kind of tethered plane. But unlike most dead-of-night inventions this one turned out to be practicable: aeronautical engineer John ten Have was able to develop Neil's idea into a reality. The first Fly by Wire in the world was opened in Paekakariki, near Wellington, in 1997, followed in 1998 by a bigger, faster version just outside Queenstown.

The aircraft is suspended by a heavy-duty cable from the focal point of a number of high-tension cables strung across a valley. The cables are attached to enormous concrete blocks and secured to the rock using bolts up to 15 metres long. The pilot is strapped face-down into the open cockpit of the wingless 4-metre aluminium rocket, which has a caged propeller at the back to provide both power and steering, powered by a 60-horsepower engine. The craft is then hauled through the flight arc until the nose is pointing vertically down.

From now on the pilot is in control. The cables holding the craft up aren't visible: all the pilot – you – can see of the aircraft is the handlebars and fully instrumented dashboard. It might as well be a jet plane. Releasing the haul rope at the same time as revving the engine gets the eight-minute flight going. The craft can fly anywhere below the supporting cables, but it can't hit anything and it can't be flown out of control. (In fact no one has ever received an injury on Fly by Wire.) Repeated hairpin turns will allow the aircraft to reach maximum speed, while a circular flight path leaves it skimming the tops of the trees.

With a maximum speed of 170 kph the Queenstown ride is, Neil Harrap claims, the fastest land-based adventure ride in the world. The Paekakariki Fly by Wire may be smaller than the Queenstown one (55 metres above the ground at its highest point as opposed to 100 metres) and slower (a fast-enough 140 kph), but it does fly within a terrifying metre or so of the ground, requires more skill because of the frequent turns, and inflicts higher G forces.

Fly by Wire tends to appeal slightly more to men than women – the speed and power feed the macho urge rather well – and more to the young than the old. You don't need to be fit, but if you're in the late stages of pregnancy, or have a heart condition or epilepsy, it's not the ride for you. The minimum age is 15, and you won't be able to fly if you weigh more than 120 kg or so. The sites are open all day, with only heavy rain causing flights to be cancelled. Take warm outdoor clothes with you, and a camera to take pictures of low-flying rockets. While you're flying you'll be far too busy to take photos, but you can have your flight recorded on video.

At the time of writing the only two Fly by Wire operations in the world were in New Zealand, but it's too good an idea not to share it, and Fly by Wire flight parks are planned for Fort Worth, Texas, and other US sites. New Zealand will, however, always be the home of Fly by Wire, and Queenstown will surely remain its most spectacular site.

Question to ask

1. How many people will be in my group and how long will I have to wait? (This applies only to Queenstown, where pilots are taken to the site in groups.)

FACE DOWN AND FLAT OUT

As the van winds up a dusty unsealed road through a farm Paul, our driver and, let's say, flight engineer, explains why the Fly by Wire site is tucked away on private land. The authorities, it seems, wouldn't let them build it in sight of a public road, for fear that drivers would be dangerously distracted by the sight of a strange little wingless flying machine sweeping across the valley. I can't say I blame them.

The whole set-up, with its cables and platform high above the valley floor, looks like something from a Bond movie. From a distance the structure looks impossibly fragile, but Paul assures me that it has been engineered to withstand far greater forces than the ride could ever impose.

A few minutes is enough to explain how it works and how to get the best out of it. It's time to put on my helmet and goggles and lie face-down in the open cockpit while Paul straps me in with a seven-point harness. I hold my hands in front of me on a set of motorcycle handlebars. Paul gives one last instruction – go hard or go home – then fires up the engine.

I discover why the harness has to be so tight as I'm winched 100 metres backwards up the side of the valley into the vertical release position. The winch stops with a jolt and with a gulp I grip the two levers on the handlebars – one to release the cable and the other for the throttle. In an instant I'm freefalling in an arc towards the bottom of the valley at 120 kph. I can feel the G forces hitting my body and when I open my mouth to give a whoop only a squeak comes out.

I'm swinging up again, looking for the road on the hillside that is my cue to do a 180° turn before the next downward journey. Full lock to the left followed by a small correction to keep my personal cruise missile straight and I'm hurtling back towards the other side of the valley. It's power-on and I'm *flying*! The wind whistles, the engine drones and back and forth I go, buzzing the spectators on the ground.

I've got one eye on the stunning Central Otago view and one eye on the speedometer. It's just like riding a swing in a playground – the higher you go the faster you go – so I try to leave each turn a little bit later. I'm starting to get a feel for it, waiting for the aircraft to slow right down and the negative Gs (that floating feeling) to kick in before giving it full lock. When I get it right the speedo flicks up to 140 kph – and it certainly *feels* that fast because at times I'm only a few metres off the ground.

Suddenly the engine cuts out: my time is up. Too soon! But I'm busting with pleasure at the flight as the aircraft swings silently down in smaller and smaller arcs. There's only one word I can think of to describe Fly by Wire: cool. Like a jetboat it's a big, powerful toy that travels at breakneck speeds, but you get to drive this one yourself. And that makes it so much more fun.

→ Fly by Wire, Queenstown.
   Phone 0-3-442 2116.

BUNGY JUMPING

Taupo Bungy

If there's one adventure activity that captures the essence of adventure tourism in New Zealand, it's bungy jumping. It was invented by a New Zealander, the first commercial operation was set up here, and for most people this is *the* place to jump.

It all began with the land divers of Pentecost Island in the South Pacific nation of Vanuatu, men who have for centuries built towers up to 25 metres high then, to prove their manhood, flung themselves off with springy vines attached to their ankles. This ritual caught the attention of the Oxford University Dangerous Sports Club in the 1970s and they made a series of illegal jumps off bridges using elastic cords designed to halt jets landing on aircraft carriers.

In the late 1980s one AJ Hackett was inspired by a video of the Dangerous Sports Club's jumps to team up with another New Zealand speed-skier, Henry Van Asch, to develop new bungy jumping technology. After extensive testing they made some leaps in France, including one from the Eiffel Tower, and in 1988 they opened the world's first full-time commercial bungy site at the Kawarau Bridge, close to Queenstown in New Zealand. Bungy jumping has since taken off around the world, but Queenstown will always be its home.

So how does bungy jumping work? First you find a high point, usually a bridge or a specially constructed platform anything from 40 to 134 metres up. Then you get a latex rubber cord of just the right thickness and length (that bit is important) and attach one end firmly to the high point, and the other to the jumper via a harness. Then you jump. And you freefall. And you bounce.

If you use a full-body harness you can jump head-first or feet-first, facing the platform or away from the platform, and when the bouncing stops you'll find yourself sitting up nicely. If you use the more traditional ankle harness you can only do a swan dive or a back dive and you generally end up dangling upside-down for a couple of minutes while the bungy crew retrieves you, either by pulling you back up to the platform or lowering you to the ground or into a boat.

If you're jumping over a river you may have the option of a water entry. The technology is accurate enough that the bungy crew can adjust the length of the cord to allow you to just touch the water with your hand, put your head in or go in up to the waist. It's up to you, but remember to bring a change of clothes. Some bungy sites offer tandem jumps, others offer night jumps. The possibilities are endless.

And what about safety? Bungy operations in this country have rigorous safety and training schemes and a code of practice has been developed in conjunction with Standards New Zealand. In more than a million jumps there has never been a bungy jumping fatality in this country, although there have been at least two injuries when the bungy cord wasn't properly attached.

BUNGY MACHINES

If you're short of time or short of money try the latest quick-fix bungy craze: reverse bungy machines. In this cross between bungy jumping and a fairground ride, up to three passengers sit in a safety cage that is attached to the tops of two towers by taut bungy cords. When the cage is released the bungy cords pull it skywards at around 160 kph and the passengers experience up to 5 Gs, then weightlessness at the top of the trajectory before gravity takes over and the ground rush starts. After about 10 bounces the ride is over and the cage is lowered back down to the ground.

There are currently operations, variously known as Bungee Rocket, Sky Screamer and Reverse Bungy, at urban sites in Auckland, Tauranga, Wellington and Christchurch.

There have been a very few reports of jumpers getting red eyes – probably as a result of pressure from breath-holding and abdominal muscle contraction – and it has been suggested that diabetics, whose retinas are particularly fragile, shouldn't jump. Certainly most operators won't take people who have any of the following conditions: pregnancy, high blood pressure, heart conditions, neurological disorders, fragile skin, neck or back problems, bone disorders and recent dislocations.

Costs start at $80, and most operators will refund your money if you chicken out *before* the cord is attached to you. For most commercial jumps children need to be at least 10 years old (for some the minimum age is 13) and weigh at least 35–40 kg. Generally there's no maximum age and no maximum weight (your average bungy cord can support the weight of around 35 people). You don't have to be fit, just healthy.

Nearly all operators can offer, at extra cost, an action video and/or photographs of your jump, and some have T-shirts that they will only sell to people who make the jump – something that will allow you to brag about your feat when you get home.

The last question has to be this: Why? What would possess anyone to pay a fairly substantial amount of money to jump off a platform? Perhaps it's a response to a primal urge, a need to feel the rush of adrenalin. Perhaps it's all about staring down death, forcing yourself to do something completely unnatural and coming away laughing. Maybe it's because, although it feels dangerous, it isn't.

Whatever the reason, it's a hell of a thing to have done.

Questions to ask

1. Do you use ankle harnesses or full-body harnesses or both?
2. What sorts of jumps or dives can I do?
3. If I change my mind about jumping, will I get my money back?
4. Can you supply transport to the bungy site?

ELASTIC FANTASTIC

It's 7 am and it's a bit of a struggle to drag myself out of bed. The reason for the early start isn't exactly working as an incentive: in a couple of hours' time I'm going to be hurtling towards the ground at something approaching 130 kph.

Maybe. I'll see when I get there.

At AJ Hackett's shop I sign the waiver and weigh in on a set of most unflattering scales. Then it's on to the bus for the 40-minute drive to the Nevis. The bleary-eyed passengers are eerily quiet. Perhaps it's the early hour. More likely we're each distracted by our own vision of imminent death – the bungy cord breaking, or being too long, or (this is my version) the cord's not being connected at the top. A knot is forming in my stomach, but I'm sure I'll be fine.

Well, maybe I will.

But before we even get to the bungy site we have our first test of nerves. The private road through a working sheep station is very steep and winding. And rough. On one side – my side – there is a precipitous unprotected drop, and as I gaze down it I contemplate the task ahead: a 134-metre plunge, around four times as far as the drop below me now.

Perhaps.

As we hit the ridge we see what we've let ourselves in for. The Nevis Highwire Bungy, with its purpose-built "jump pod" suspended from 380-metre cables spanning the Nevis Gorge, is unique. It is also the highest bungy in New Zealand, more than three times the height of the original bungy on the Kawarau Bridge. The fact that the gorge funnels to a mere 30 metres at river level only adds to the impression of extreme height. From our vantage point on the ridge it's a long way down, there's no doubt about that – and we're going to be experiencing every cubic centimetre of air between the pod and the bottom of the valley.

At least that's the idea.

I'm reweighed and this time my weight is written on the back of my hand with a marker pen. No opportunity for coyness here. I jump into a full-body harness, then it's into a cable car for a gentle, gravity-powered ride to the jump pod. There's plenty of room in the pod for all of us: nine jumpers – eight blokes plus me – sundry girlfriends to take the photos, and three bungy crew.

We're jumping in reverse order of weight (there are five bungy cords of different thicknesses), so it looks like I'm going to be the last. It's quite a wait, long enough for the nerves to set in properly. One by one the other jumpers depart while we watch them through the vertigo-inducing clear strip in the floor of the pod. One by one they reappear full of smiles and swear words. That's going to be me soon.

I think.

At last it's my turn. My stomach churns as I settle into the comfy chair to get clipped on to the bungy cord at the waist and at the ankles. I try to laugh lightly at the jump master's jokes, but the laughter is hollow. Then it's famous last words to the video camera, shuffle over to the gang plank, wave at another video camera outside and, no time to think, the bungy crew are yelling, "Five, four, three, two–"

Before they get to one I'm off, plunging into the chasm, plummeting head-first, every muscle in my body tensed. Throat too tight to scream, lips peeled back over my teeth, I'm eyeballing the river as it hurtles, spinning and spiralling, towards me at 130 kph. What seemed like a slow, graceful fall by the others *feels* exactly the opposite – a shaky, hand-held video on fast-forward. This is very serious ground rush.

Four or five seconds of freefall are over in what seems like half a second and the bungy cord kicks in harshly at my ankles. A moment later I'm heading back towards the pod for my second burst of freefall, although it's more of a floating sensation this time. At the top of the second bounce I release my feet from the bungy cord (something not instinctively natural – but then there's nothing remotely natural about this whole experience) by yanking a cord, my feet drop down and I'm sitting in my harness ready for the ride back up.

And as I clamber back into the pod I'm full of smiles and swear words, just like everyone else. "How was it?" the jump master asks me. "Better when it stopped," I reply.

At the end of the four-hour trip I have the option to buy a video of my jump, action photos and a T-shirt sold only to jumpers, but I end up with none of these. Instead I take home an achy bruise on my left ankle and my own at-no-extra-cost tape of the valley floor rushing at me running on a loop inside my head.

→ AJ Hackett Bungy, Queenstown.
Freephone 0800 BUNGY JUMP (0800 286 495).

EARTH ADVENTURES

ADVENTURE CAVING

Ratings			
■■☐☐☐	to	■■■■☐	Adrenalin Rush
■■■☐☐	to	■■■■■	Personal Input

Black Water "Rafting"®

Adventure caving – or potholing, as it is known in the UK – using modern climbing and abseiling equipment has been around as sport for 50 or 60 years, although we have for thousands of years overcome our perfectly reasonable fear of dark, slimy, mysterious places – homes to trolls, gnomes, hobgoblins and taniwha – to explore caves.

For most visitors to New Zealand's North Island, Waitomo Caves appears somewhere on the itinerary. The stunning show caves, with their spectacular limestone formations and enchanting glowworms, have been a tourist attraction for well over a century, ever since Fred Mace and Tane Tinorau made the first exploration of the Glowworm Cave in 1887. The show caves are immensely popular with young and old – but although the New Zealand caving experience may have begun there, it doesn't need to end there.

The Waitomo area is honeycombed with cave systems and for the last 15 years or so some of the less easily accessible – and less tame – caves have been opened up to adventure cavers on a commercial basis. Adventure caving trips are also available in caves on the West Coast of the South Island and in Nelson, and some independent adventure guides will arrange them.

There are a number of possible elements in commercially run caving trips. Often there's an abseil (rappel) to get into the cave and there may be other abseils within the caves themselves; these vary in height from just a few metres to 275 metres at Harwoods Hole. You might jump 2 or 3 metres into a pool, slide down a chute or swim for a while in icy water (whatever the season and however thick your wetsuit, you're going to get cold in an underground river).

Some caving trips include cave tubing or rafting, in which you float along an underground river in an inner tube. You might have to squeeze and squirm through some fairly tight spaces, and do some climbing up a ladder, up a rock wall or up a waterfall. A few trips include a Tyrolean traverse, in which you ride across a chasm dangling below a tight rope. And almost always there will be the very particular treat of a glowworm display.

Adventure caving is, by definition, a fairly demanding experience and you'll need to have full mobility and average to good fitness. You won't enjoy it at all if you have phobias about enclosed spaces or darkness – and you won't get very far in the dimly lit environment if you have night blindness. For some of the less challenging trips there is a minimum age of eight, but for more technical trips children may need to be 15 or 16.

A good qualification to look for in a guide is a New Zealand Outdoor Instructors Association caving award, but many companies rely on in-house training. The more demanding the trip, the more important the ratio of guides to customers is going to be. On a tough trip, any more than six clients to one guide is going to make things difficult. A smaller group will also mean shorter traffic jams at the abseils or tricky sections. As far as safety goes, although many recreational cavers have died world-wide and there has been one drowning on a tourist trip in New Zealand, commercial caving in this country is done under very controlled circumstances and injuries worse than a twisted ankle are rare.

When commercial caving began 15 years ago the clients were mostly young backpackers prepared to rough it to get a true adventure experience on the cheap. These days many customers are willing to pay for creature comforts and some caving companies are happy to cater

GLOWWORMS

Glowworms are a unique and magical feature of damp, dark caves in south-east Australia and New Zealand, and nowhere are they more numerous than in the shimmering constellations at Waitomo. They're not related to the European glowworm, and they're not actually worms: in fact they're the larvae of the fungus gnat. Their distinctive luminescence is designed to lure insects into a trap of sticky hanging threads. It's important not to touch glowworms or their glistening threads, and shining a bright torch directly on them is likely to make them stop glowing.

to their needs. Trips range widely in price, from $65 for a no-frills half-day trip to nearly $1000 for a full-day heli-caving experience. In the end you get what you pay for, and if you're prepared to get your own clothes and shoes wet or muddy, for example, it's not hard to cut costs.

Caves can be quite magical places – if they're your thing – so if you do take a caving trip don't forget to pause along the way and enjoy your surroundings. Between abseils, squeezes and freezing swims, take the time to examine – but not touch – the stalagmites and stalactites, including hollow straw stalactites, admire the cave "coral" and other strange formations, and look out for the fossils of sea creatures from millions of years ago.

Questions to ask

1. How many customers will there be on the trip?
2. What is the ratio of guides to customers?
3. If there is abseiling, do I control my own descent or will the guide lower me?
4. Do you supply boots or do I have to wear my own shoes?
5. Do you have hot showers?

A LEAP IN THE DARK

There's something about gear, you know. All that technical stuff – harnesses, helmets, carabiners, ropes – has a mysterious allure. It makes you feel intrepid, expert, a serious adventurer. Or maybe it's just a fetish thing.

Either way, adventure caving beats all-comers when it comes to gear: we spend a good half-hour at the Black Water "Rafting" base just getting dressed. First there's the two-piece wetsuit, neoprene booties for warmth and plastic boots for strength, then harness, abseil rack, cowstail and carabiner, followed by a helmet with lamp and a bulky, heavy battery on a waistband.

First-up our guides Debs and Hohepa take us through a bit of abseiling training. We learn to control our speed using the friction device on our harnesses – and are reassured that if we lose control Hohepa can stop us dead (poor choice of words, I think) with one yank on the rope.

From the top all I can see of the 35-metre entrance shaft, called a tomo, is darkness. When I begin my descent into the abyss I discover that in places the smooth limestone tomo is very narrow, and I have to squirm a little to get through. It comes as something of a surprise, and it's the first of many surprises. This may be quite deliberate: it doesn't give us the opportunity to baulk at things that, given time and choice, we might not have had the nerve to do.

But all that's ahead of us. We make our way down a narrow passage, pausing to admire the tiny, delicate stalactites that hang from the dripping ceiling. Before long Hohepa tells us to clip our cowstails (short safety ropes) to a running rope on the wall. We all turn off our lamps and pitch darkness envelops us.

A moment later there's a loud mechanical hum, and a human howl that echoes and disappears into the distance. Debs has gone but it's not clear where or how. One by one the people ahead of me disappear in similar style, some with a holler and some with a scream. When my turn comes Hohepa clips my harness onto a cable and pushes me into a darkness that is so intense it sucks me in. I whoop as I hurtle into the jaws of hell then come to a swinging halt at the bottom. I find that, although it's the middle of the day and I'm a long way underground, it's a starry night – constellations of glowworms twinkle above my head.

We stop for lunch and to throw morsels to the big, fat eel that lurks in the river below. Then we each grab an inflated inner tube for a bit of black water (as opposed to whitewater) rafting. With no warning or time to think, we're leaping into the still river a couple of metres below, bum in tube, feet out, to hit the water with a deafening smack.

Shit it's cold. The shivering begins.

We warm up by paddling our tubes, and occasionally walking, down the river, pausing from time to time to examine a fossil or a speleological (that's a damn fine word) feature. After a while we form a chain as we sit in our tubes, then turn off our lamps. The glowworms' lanterns all around us seem much brighter than the stars in the sky.

Through the darkness Hohepa pulls our human chain back the way we came. Distantly a faint, sweet melody echoes: Debs, like the sirens of Greek mythology, is calling us into her lair. I'm struck by the ethereal song that serenades us through endless galaxies of glowworms, but around me the chatter continues irritatingly. These people, I think, just don't *get* it.

When we rejoin Debs we turn on our lamps, leave the inner tubes behind and work our way upstream. A good thing too: the cold is really beginning to set in. When I stand up after swimming for a while the water inside my wetsuit, heated by my body, drains out of my sleeves. There's a lovely warmth as it exits . . . but hey that's *my* warmth, and I can't afford to be giving it away like this!

The underground river offers all sorts of different terrain: sometimes we pick our way on foot over smooth, slippery rocks, sometimes we swim, occasionally we crawl. When we come to a watery "squeeze", a place where the cave constricts dramatically, we all dutifully squirm through on our stomachs – before we realise that we could have just walked through a large arch right beside it.

From time to time we stop to eat a piece of chocolate, check out a fossil or tickle an eel. We clamber up small waterfalls, zip face-first down a slide and try not to hit our heads as we wriggle through tiny passages. Never knowing what's around the corner, I'm feeling like a real adventurer.

A waterfall roars in the distance. The noise turns into a thundering as I crawl round the final corner. I work my way around, and then through, the crashing cascade – and then *up* it! This is nerve-wracking. I worry about my plastic boots sliding off the slick rock, I worry about the pounding water throwing me off balance, and I worry about all the jagged rocks waiting to break my body when I fall.

But once again we're given no option by our guides, and no time to think. I follow the rest of the group up and it feels surprisingly secure with Debs showing me where to put my hands and feet. After one last crawl I get my reward – daylight! Climbing out through the small opening into the brightness of the afternoon feels strangely like a rebirth.

I immediately set off up the hill looking for a sunny patch, peeling off layers as I go. Hot showers, hot soup and bagels await us back at the base. It's great to be warm again.

→ Black Water "Rafting"®, Waitomo.
Freephone 0800 CAVING (0800 228 464).

LUGE

The luge is yet another fine product of legendary Kiwi ingenuity, yet another world first. When Skyline opened its luge run in Rotorua in 1985 it was the first of its type and it's still one of only a few like it in the world – the only others are in Japan.

Now don't confuse the New Zealand luge with the super-sleek toboggan ridden by crazy Teutonic types at the Winter Olympics. The name and the crazy drivers may be the same but this luge has wheels and the track is concrete or clay instead of ice. Although it has its dangers, it's also not to be confused with the utterly lunatic street luge, in which racers lie on modified skateboards and hurtle feet-first down steep, winding streets.

The New Zealand luge – at least the three-wheeled Skyline version – is more like a tiny gravity-powered racecar. Its unique steering and braking system allows the rider full control through the handlebars. You can go as fast or as slow as you like down the winding reinforced concrete track, so you get to choose how much of a rush you get. Both Skyline sites, Rotorua and Queenstown, have a couple of tracks: one sedate, scenic track and one fast or advanced track for the speed junkies. A chairlift takes riders back up to the top.

Another version of luge can be found at Papamoa Adventure Park. If Skyline is the formula one of gravity luge then Papamoa is the rally version. The cart looks more like a genuine racing cart: it has four wheels, a steering wheel and a roll cage, and it drifts around corners on the dirt track (another world first) like a real rally car. The owners claim top speeds of 90 kph are possible. Enough to get anyone's blood going.

LIVE AND LET LUGE

There are two distinct groups of luge riders at the Skyline Luge in Queenstown – the folk who buy a single ticket and take a leisurely trip down the Scenic Track, pausing along the way to take photos of the entrancing view of Lake Wakatipu through the pines, and then there are the death-or-glory speedsters determined to make it to the bottom of the Fast Track in record time. I'll let you guess which category I fall into.

But before the downhill, there has to be the uphill, which in this case is a ride in the super-steep gondola to the Skyline complex at the top of Bobs Peak in Queenstown. Here the views of the ragged peaks of the Remarkables Range are, um, remarkable.

At the top of the luge I get a quick introduction to driving the cart: go, stop, steer and park, all using the handlebars. Then I strap on a bike helmet, engage the seat belt, and gravity takes me off down the concrete track. The first run of the day is a compulsory jaunt down the Scenic Track to get the hang of steering and braking. It's hard to get into too much trouble on this gently sloping track, and the cart seems to be pretty simple to control. It's clear from the start, though, that getting the corners right is going to be the hardest part.

A chairlift takes me back to the top for a run at the serious stuff: the Fast Track. I soon discover that it's steeper than the Scenic Track, with some nasty dips and tight, banked corners. It is designed to throw riders off their carts – or so it seems to me as I screech my way down it.

I make it in one piece to the bottom, where the lift operator informs me that the all-comers record for the Fast Track is 46.5 seconds, which by my calculations means an average speed of close to 60 kph. Well I'm not doing anything near that speed – thank God. The liftie also gives me some tips for maximum efficiency: leave off the brakes altogether, and give the cart full lock and a heavy body lean on the corners.

My inner rally driver accepts the challenge and for the next few runs I find I'm pushing it harder and harder, getting faster and faster. It's pretty hairy at times, and it takes a whole lot of self-control to leave the brakes alone as I career towards the corners. After five runs and a few near-misses in which I come perilously close to rolling the cart I decide to call it quits. I pose no threat to the record.

→ Skyline Luge, Queenstown. Phone 0-3-441 0101.

ZORB

Ratings

■■■☐☐   Adrenalin Rush

☐☐☐☐☐   to   ■■☐☐☐   Personal Input

Zorb

What's big, round and bouncy and inflated with air? Right, a beach ball. What's really big, round and bouncy, inflated with air and has a person in it? A Zorb!

    Let me explain. This unlikely New Zealand phenomenon, invented by Dwane van der Sluis and Andrew Akers in the mid-1990s, really *is* a giant beach ball. It's a 3-metre clear PVC sphere inflated with around 13 cubic metres of air, with a small entrance tunnel leading to an inner sphere suspended by nearly 1000 internal ties. The Zorbonaut climbs into the inner sphere, harnesses himself or herself in, and the ride begins.

The Zorb is sent rolling down a slope and the Zorbonaut rotates with it, protected from lumps and bumps by a 70-centimetre cushion of air. Centrifugal force pins the Zorbonaut to the inside of the Zorb – except that at the top of each rotation gravity intervenes and there's a brief feeling of weightlessness.

The Wet Zorb, also known as the Wash Cycle, is the Dry Zorb with water – pretty much like a front-loading washing machine. The Zorbonaut shares the inner sphere with a bucketful of water and, with no harness, slips, slides, flips and sloshes around on the way down. If you want the gentlest possible ride you can just sit at the bottom and the Zorb will rotate around you – but if you want a challenge there's a prize of a free T-shirt to anyone who can run inside the Zorb all the way without falling over. You can even put two people inside the Wet Zorb.

Zorbing is the sort of strange, wonderful but supremely simple adventure activity that could only be invented by Kiwis. It is possible in all but the most extreme weather conditions, and everyone from two-year-olds (in a special flat-ground Kids Zorb) to the elderly is welcome to give it a try. Well, almost everyone: if you are pregnant, have a heart condition, have neck or back problems, or weigh more than 160 kg, it may not be possible. And as adventure tourism activities go it's safe: injuries are almost unheard of.

It looks like it would make you sick, but although the Zorb can reach speeds of 50 kph, the rotation is quite slow and relaxed. No one has ever thrown up inside the Zorb – but if you're thinking of using the Zorb as a hangover cure be warned that a couple of lads doing just that have lost their breakfast after the ride was over.

ON A ROLL

From the bottom the hill looks long and steep. From the top of the longest ramp it looks worse. I'm having doubts – I'm the sort of person who likes to have a bit of control over what's happening in my world, and the idea of rolling unstoppably and unsteerably down a hill isn't looking all that appealing.

Dave hoses off the somewhat muddy Zorb (all the better to see the view) then I dive as enthusiastically as I can through the entrance tunnel. I lie down on a comfortable pad, poke my toes into a couple of loops, strap myself in and grab hold of another couple of loops above my head. I brace myself.

Dave pushes the Zorb off the platform and I'm slowly on my way, heels over head. The light of the sky is replaced by the dark of the ground, then the light reappears. As the Zorb picks up speed the feeling is unique and quite surreal. The ride is surprisingly soft but the ever-moving horizon makes me feel dizzy and disoriented and, after a couple of rotations, ever so slightly sick.

Just when I'm starting to get used to the sensation, the Zorb slows and stops as it enters the bowl at the bottom of the hill. I lie still in my harness for a while, waiting for my brain to stop spinning and my stomach to settle.

That was very, very strange.

→ Zorb Rotorua. Phone 0-7-357 5100.

ROPES COURSE

Ratings	
■■■□□	Adrenalin Rush
■■■■■	Personal Input

Rock n Ropes

Ropes courses were originally inspired by military obstacle courses, but they don't have the macho strength elements or the crawling through mud under cargo nets. They consist of a series of supervised challenges designed to test teamwork and individual commitment. These challenges are – surprise, surprise – based around the use of ropes or cables, and to do them you don't need to have great fitness or strength, just a sense of fun and adventure.

Sometimes called challenge ropes courses or confidence courses, they've been around in various forms for a long time, but really took off in the 1970s and 1980s, when "experiential training" and "challenge by choice" became buzz concepts in the educational world. Usually it's groups from educational institutions or, in recent years, from companies looking to encourage teamwork amongst staff, that have access to ropes courses. There is one ropes course in New Zealand, though, that seven days a week gives individuals the chance to test their nerve: Rock'n Ropes in Taupo.

Like most ropes courses, Rock'n Ropes has both high and low elements. The low elements are less than 1.5 metres from the ground, while the high elements can be as high as 15 metres. For the high course helmets, harnesses and climbing ropes provide protection should you fall. The result is that, despite feeling scary, the high elements are if anything safer than the low ones. Gear failure notwithstanding, the worst injury you're likely to get is a graze or a bruise.

If you decide to take on the high ropes course you'll need to bring with you loose, comfortable clothes and lace-up sports shoes, as well as sunscreen in summer. This activity is not really very weather-dependent, although high winds, heavy rain or lightning would be a problem.

Ropes courses hold very different rewards for different people. If, like me, you don't have a problem with heights and you're used to entrusting your life to a belayer holding a length of rope, a few hours on the ropes course will be challenging but fun. At the other end of the spectrum, if you're nervous about heights and don't consider yourself a "physical" person or lack confidence in your abilities, you may find high ropes activities, especially the giant trapeze, extremely draining both mentally and physically – but your sense of achievement and exhilaration at completing or even attempting them will be far greater.

The thrill of doing a ropes course comes from doing it all yourself – unlike other adventure tourism activities you're not being chucked off a bridge, or guided down a river by a whitewater expert, or driven through a canyon by a jetboat driver with hundreds of hours of driving time behind him. There's supervision and safety equipment, but it's up to you to make the most of the experience.

FLYING FOX

Ropes courses often include a flying fox (also known as a zip line or, disturbingly, death slide), but they pop up in all sorts of other places too. A ride on a heavy-duty flying fox – as opposed to the kids' version you can find in adventure playgrounds – involves climbing up to a high platform, making yourself secure via a harness and a safety line, then taking hold of a handle that runs along a cable that disappears down and away into the distance. Next you step off the platform and squeal your way down the cable, gathering speed as you go before being brought to a none-too-gentle halt by a brake at the bottom.

The rides can go for anything from 200 metres to 500 metres, and one operator claims a maximum speed of more than 100 kph. The whole experience is usually over in a matter of seconds, making it a good quick-fix adventure thrill if you're short of time.

LEARNING THE ROPES

As we gaze at the high – imposingly high – ropes course Angela, our very young, very tanned and very blonde instructor, tells us we're going to be responsible for each other's safety. It occurs to me that this will be our first challenge: overcoming a perfectly natural and sensible reluctance to entrust our lives to a complete stranger. At any rate, to this end we learn how to belay each other on a rope, something that requires a certain amount of dexterity and co-ordination. It's ballroom dancing for the hands: one, two, three, four – forward, side, together, forward.

Mission one is a two-wire bridge 10 metres above the ground, with one cable for the feet and one at chest height. As I shimmy along sideways, pushing my hands away from my body – "Whatever you do, don't lean back!" shouts Angela – there is a disturbing wobbling underfoot. But the further I go the easier it gets and, like William and Kate, I get safely to the end. Mission one complete.

Mission two is a three-wire Burma bridge, which it seems to me ought to be easier – but it isn't. As I step splay-footed along one cable, clutching the other two with my hands, a huge, rhythmic oscillation begins. I can't imagine a tightrope walker ever doing this without handrails.

After comfortably conquering a rickety bridge and a narrow, round, beam-like catwalk we get a shock to the system: the multi-vine. There are two wires 2.5 metres or more apart vertically, with ropes of varying lengths hanging from the top one at intervals of about 2 to 2.5 metres. To get your hand on the next "vine" along you need to hold on to the last one with one hand, get as far along the wire as you can, then reach out with your free hand.

William is in no doubt: "There's no way I can do this." And I have to say, for all my gung-ho girl-power attitude, I'm not sure I can either. The vines seem impossibly far apart. But William does it, though not without massive wobbling and shaking. Kate's next and she's not so lucky. Her technique's better, but she hasn't got the stamina. After a few minutes of desperate grabbing and hanging she hasn't got the strength to go on, and for the first time one of us doesn't

---

GIANT SWING

Like the idea of a bungy jump, but it sounds a bit too scary? Well how about taking a swing instead of a jump? A couple of operators – including Rock'n Ropes at Taupo – can launch you on a giant swing, which is a bit like bridge swinging from a purpose-built structure.

You're linked via a harness to steel cables attached to the tops of a pair of high towers or poles. You then climb or are winched up to a high point on the swing's arc and jump or are released to whistle down and round to within a couple of metres of the ground before swinging up the other side to experience a moment of weightlessness before falling, swinging and spinning back again.

The impressive Swoop at Rotorua is the highest tech swing in New Zealand. Up to three riders (the greater the weight, the better the ride) are zipped into full hang gliding harnesses, hauled backwards to 40 metres off the ground, then swing head-first at anything up to 130 kph. It's a great rush, but gentle, short and not too terrifying.

complete a task. We're all disappointed. Now I'm really worried. Kate has been my role model, jumping in feet-first and attacking every challenge with gusto. If she can't do it . . . and she's taller than me, with longer arms . . . will I be able to?

Well I do, but only just. I bring some of my rock-climbing skills to bear, hanging off straight arms and spreading my feet wide apart to give a solid base. As soon as I catch the bottom of each vine with my right hand I move it as high up the vine as I can, to give stability. And that's what gets me to the end – that and brute strength. By the end my left arm is throbbing with the workout it has done and my hand is frozen closed. But I've done it. And I'm proud of myself.

There is worse to come: the feature of the high ropes course, the giant trapeze. Climb up a 13-metre pole and onto the top of it, then launch yourself forwards and upwards to a trapeze and catch it if you can. William, who up till now has noisily predicted disaster at every turn, is strangely quiet, but quickly volunteers to go first. He spends an age making the move from the small metal footholds on the side of the pole to the top. From 20 metres away we can see his whole body trembling and the sweat glistening. After a few frozen minutes he commits himself and suddenly he's on the top. It's a few minutes more before he works himself up into making the leap. At his request we all count backwards from five, bungy style – and off he goes, and makes the bar. He hoots and hollers with joy!

Kate is inspired by his success, and makes it too. So that leaves me. I race up the pole and for a while contemplate the distinctly dodgy move onto the flat top of the pole. There is nothing to hang on to, nothing to steady myself on. I get both hands and one foot on top, then take a deep breath and drag the other foot up. I squat precariously for a couple of seconds, then stand up. I'm on top of a 13-metre pole with nothing but air all around. The pole sways beneath me – the wind seems stronger up here – and the trapeze seems ridiculously far away. On a count of three I'm flying through the air reaching for the trapeze and next thing I know I have the bar and I'm screeching with excitement. I'm enjoying it so much I don't want to let go.

The final challenge is the giant swing. I am belayed up to a platform 15 metres off the ground, where Angela links my harness to cables attached to a couple of towers. I step off the platform and what starts out as a yahoo rapidly turns into a blood-curdling death squeal as I reach terminal velocity – or what seems like it – before the swing kicks in and I pendulum for a while.

It's kinda fun, kinda not – like most adventure activities it's better in retrospect.

→ Rock'n Ropes, Taupo.
   Freephone 0800 244 508.

GUIDED ADVENTURES

Guy Channer

New Zealand is known the world over for the quality of its mountain guides, and wonderfully experienced, well-qualified, multi-talented creatures they are. Depending on qualifications and experience, mountain guides can lead all sorts of expeditions, from rock climbing, mountaineering and canyoning to ski-touring and glacier exploration. If they have the relevant awards, some can also take you caving, rafting, kayaking or paragliding . . . the possibilities are endless.

Guides differ from most other adventure operators in that you don't have to select from a menu of trips and activities at fixed times and at set prices. Many guides work on their own or in very small businesses, and your adventure experience is generally tailored to fit your needs. There are a number of qualifications to look for in a guide. The most highly qualified have UIAGM (International Union of Mountain Guides Associations) status, while members of the New Zealand Mountain Guides Association (NZMGA) are nearly as well regarded. The New Zealand Outdoor Instructors Association (NZOIA) also administers highly respected awards in several disciplines.

Week-long mountaineering courses and guided ascents of major summits both in New Zealand and overseas may be on offer from mountain guides, but it is one-day adventure experiences suitable for beginners that are covered in this book. Some of these, like canyoning and whitewater rafting, are covered elsewhere, but following is a quick rundown of specialist activities that may be available.

ABSEILING

Ratings	
■■■☐☐	Adrenalin Rush
■■■■☐	Personal Input

Abseiling, which is also known as rappelling, was invented many years ago by mountaineers as a quick and easy way to descend mountains and steep rock or ice faces. Once a necessity, it has now become a sport in its own right, one providing an appealing challenge for those wanting to test their mettle and any fear of heights while learning a fairly quickly acquired skill.

After instruction and possibly some practice abseils on low-angle slopes, the guide sets up an anchor system at the top of a cliff (it might be as high as 100 metres), then attaches the ropes. You put on a helmet and a harness and after instruction the guide secures you to the rope with a friction device that will allow you to control the speed of your descent down the rope.

Then it's time to begin. And that's the hardest part: going over the edge. Every fibre of your body is telling you that stepping backwards into thin air is a mistake. While your brain understands that the equipment can hold 40 times your weight, your instincts are telling you not to risk it. But you'll do it anyway and once you're there, making shuffling steps down the cliff face while feeding rope through the friction device, you might even enjoy it. Don't forget to stop and look at the view!

Try not to worry too much: there's hardly anything that can go wrong. In the extremely unlikely event that you lose control – you panic and let go, say, or faint with excitement – your guide will quickly stop your descent by, depending on the technique being used, either pulling the abseiling rope taut from below, or locking off a safety rope from the top.

If you enjoy the basic abseils you might like to try something else. An abseil from an overhang offers quite an experience: hanging on a rope in mid-air is very different from working your way down a face. Rap jumping, where you descend face down, is completely different again.

Abseiling is not half so dangerous as it looks or feels. As long as all the safety equipment is properly maintained and set up, and your harness and carabiners are properly done up – a qualified instructor will take care of all this – the most likely source of serious injury is getting too close to the edge of the cliff while other people are abseiling.

You don't need to be very fit, and age is no barrier: some guides can take people as young as five or as old as 90. Wear warm, loose, comfortable clothes, and sensible shoes that you can walk a reasonable distance in and that you don't mind getting muddy. If your hands are very delicate you may want to take bike gloves or gardening gloves to protect them.

Questions to ask

1. Do you provide gloves?
2. How many different abseils will we do, and what are their heights?
3. Can I try rap jumping if I want to?
4. How far will we have to walk?

ROCK CLIMBING

Rock climbing, although it has a lot in common with abseiling, has an extra dimension to it: you go up as well as down. This more than doubles the demands.

The sport of rock climbing was developed around 130 years ago in the European Alps, and you might say it came about by necessity. The first great age of mountaineering had come to an end because all the major Alpine summits had been achieved, so the mountaineers had to find new challenges. Up till then they'd just taken the easiest route up each peak, which generally meant climbing through snow and ice; now the challenge was to pioneer harder and harder routes to the top – and this often meant going up sheer rock faces.

New Zealand is known for the quality of its rock climbing, and there are many very classy crags. There is good climbing to be had in the central North Island, but the South Island has the really exceptional climbing areas, from Nelson in the north to the very popular crags around Wanaka.

A rock climbing guide should be able to provide all the equipment necessary for beginners, from ropes and harnesses to helmets and, in some cases, rock shoes. It's worth using these very tight shoes, even if it means hiring some from an outdoors shop: they make life a lot easier. The guide will take you to an area that's suited to your ability (or lack of it), set up a safety system, teach you how to keep yourself and your climbing partner secure on a "top-rope", and teach you the basics of technique. Most trips take a full day, and you'll probably have to take your own water and refreshments. Wear warm, loose clothing and shoes you can walk a fair distance in.

Rock climbing is an addictive activity. The initial challenge may be to get over a fear of falling, but you'll find that there's much more to climbing than that. While you're concentrating on finding your way up the rock face you're totally focused on the here and now and everything else just slips away. Sometimes it's so absorbing that you don't even feel pain. It's definitely a mind game – it's a misconception that you need to be very strong and fit to enjoy it – and women often pick up the skills faster than men.

Before the development of modern safety equipment and belaying techniques rock climbing was properly dangerous, but things have changed since the days of hobnail boots and hemp ropes tied around the waist. Now, although rock climbing may look and sometimes feel scary, if you're top-roping under the supervision of an expert you are very, very unlikely to get hurt. To be sure you're in good hands, go with a UIAGM or NZMGA climbing guide, or an instructor with the NZOIA rock climbing award.

Questions to ask

1. Do you provide rock shoes?
2. Will all the people in my group be at the same level of ability?
3. How far do we have to walk to get to the climbing area?
4. Will we stay in the same place all the time or will we go to more than one area?

LIFE ON THE LEDGE

Our guide Jeremaia, a young man with a passion for the outdoors, greets us at the Mountain Works shop. There are four punters – Jen, Harry, Peggy and me – all eager to test ourselves on Queenstown's rock. None of the others has done any rock climbing before, but they all bring with them ambition and the "go-for-it attitude" requisite in adventure tourism. We sort out equipment and then head out for an introductory session at a handy roadside cliff.

We climb into our gear – comfortable harnesses, good quality rock shoes (snug-fitting shoes with special rubber soles) and helmets for safety – then learn how to tie ourselves onto the rope and how to belay each other on the stretchy ropes that will save us if we fall. Everyone pays very close attention, especially to the bit where Jeremaia tells us that one end of the rope is called the "dead" end because if the belayer lets it go, the climber's dead.

Now we can start climbing, on a route that's not too hard. We're working in teams of three: one person climbing, one belaying and one backing up the belayer in case things should go wrong. This is *really* serious stuff and it's important we get it right – so we're glad that Jeremaia's a good teacher, relaxed and knowledgeable, who doesn't overload us with more information than we need.

It takes a while for us to get used to the idea of trusting our shoes to stay on tiny ledges or steeply sloping, smooth rock, but amazingly they do. We learn, with gentle guidance from Jeremaia, to use our legs more than our arms so that we don't wear ourselves out. We're all pleased with our first climb of the day, but there's no chance to bask in the glory because we're soon off to our next, tougher challenge.

Arawata crag is up a narrow, rough-as-guts, four-wheel-drive track just out of Queenstown. The road only goes so far, though, and after a quick bite of lunch we hoist our packs onto our backs for the 15-minute slog up a steep, slimy track. Jeremaia brightly informs us that it's a good warm-up for the climbing to come.

Our second climb of the day is considerably more demanding than the first. Still, we're getting the hang of it and when we get to the top our efforts are rewarded with an immense sense of satisfaction – and quite sensational views over the lake and town. I feel at home on

ICE CLIMBING

If you want to feel like a real mountaineer, you can try this type of climbing in winter in a number of mountain areas, and year-round on the South Island's West Coast glaciers. Technical ice climbing (don't confuse it with less challenging things like glacier walks) involves an ice face, a climber, a pair of crampons, two pick-like ice tools and a safety rope.

You hold yourself on the ice by kicking the spiky fronts of the crampons into the ice as well as driving the points of the ice tools in above your head. Then you start moving up. Simple as that. You'll find that it takes astonishingly little to hold you safely on even a vertical ice wall: just a centimetre of ice axes and crampons in the ice will do it. But don't worry – there's always the rope to catch you if you fall.

Ice climbing is quite demanding and can be tiring for beginners, but it's also exciting and very rewarding – and makes for really impressive photos. It isn't an activity for kids. You'll have to be in good health and pretty fit, and can't afford to be overweight. Go with an NZMGA guide and take warm and waterproof clothing and food if it is not provided.

the rock and I think that everyone else is taking things well in their stride until Jen mentions that the tiring muscles, trembling legs and holding on to tiny flakes and ledges of rock 15 metres above the ground almost got to her and she nearly peed her pants with fear (her belayer is more than grateful that she didn't). Later Peggy, tight-lipped, asks us to stop talking about hospitals while she's climbing.

For every new climb we attempt Jeremaia ups the ante. The atmosphere is laid back – there's time to talk, to joke – but the climbing is ever more challenging and each time we apply skills learnt on the last route. We're learning fast, setting our own goals and being responsible for our own safety, but all under the watchful eye of an experienced guide.

We finish the day with a more difficult route that will be a challenge for us all. First Jeremaia makes his way up it methodically, explaining what he's doing as he goes. He's a good climber but, worryingly, he's not making it look exactly easy.

Harry's the first to attempt to breach the final frontier. Jeremaia knows it's going to be tough, so has instituted a "three falls and you're out" policy, but Harry's content to give up after two falls. His arms are pumped out, shaking with exhaustion, and he's lost one too many layers of skin from his fingertips. Jen uses up her three falls pretty quickly but is happy enough to come down too.

Peggy is a revelation. What she lacks in size she makes up for in determination. She's watched the others and learnt from their mistakes, and she quickly gets further than either. She's a woman on a mission – disappointed she had to give up on the previous climb without getting to the top, this time she's going to get there come hell or high water.

She climbs, she falls, she climbs, she falls, again and again, refusing to come down after her three falls, until she just has nothing left. She's angry at her body for letting her down, and angry at the crag for not letting her up. She feels defeated but she'll be coming back for more.

She has caught the climbing bug. I can tell – I've got it too.

→ Mountain Works, Queenstown. Phone 0-3-442 7329.

BRIDGE SWINGING

The curious phenomenon of bridge swinging was invented in England's Lake District by a Cumbrian man. From 1984 a bunch of thrillseekers called the Brigsteer Bridgeswingers pioneered and developed the sport, and in recent years bridge swinging has spread around the world.

The sport uses a dynamic (read stretchy) climbing rope rather than a bungy cord, which is much bouncier. The rope is slung under a high bridge. One end of the rope is attached securely to one side of the bridge, and the other is attached, equally securely, to the "swinger" on the other side. He or she dives off, freefalls for a moment, then pendulums under the bridge and out the other side, experiencing a moment of weightlessness at the end of each swing. The swinger can reach speeds of 70 kph.

There aren't any full-time commercial sites in this country, but some qualified mountain guides have the right equipment, technical expertise, understanding of safety issues and local knowledge to take you bridge swinging. Although the rope has "give" in it, so there shouldn't be too much of a jerk when it takes, bridge swinging is not a good idea if you're pregnant or have back problems.

WATER ADVENTURES

Rivers are graded according to difficulty, although grading is fairly subjective and a subject of some disagreement. The gradings given in the listings in this book are as supplied by each operator, and it has to be said that some of them seem to crank up the numbers to make a river seem more impressive. The grade of a river will also vary according to riverflow. All in all, gradings should be taken with a pinch of salt. Here they are:

1 Moving water with a few riffles and small waves. No obstructions.
2 Easy rapids with waves up to 1 metre. Water may slosh over the deck or into the raft, but with no real force.
3 Rapids with high irregular waves and narrow passages. (This is where whitewater starts and things get interesting.)
4 Difficult rapids. (This is very exciting and scary.)
5 Very difficult, long and violent rapids. (This is not just exciting, it's damn terrifying.)
6 Extreme, dangerous and only for experts. Not commercially rafted.

CANYONING

Ratings		
■■■□□ to ■■■■■		Adrenalin Rush
■■■□□ to ■■■■■		Personal Input

Canyonz

Say the word "canyoning" to most people (or "canyoneering" to Americans) and the first thing they'll say is: "Weren't all those people who died in Switzerland canyoning? Isn't it really dangerous?" The answer is yes. And no. Yes, a large group was killed in a canyoning disaster in Switzerland a while ago, but no, it doesn't have to be dangerous.

If you don't know what canyoning actually entails, think of it as caving in the open air. The object is to follow a river downstream through a high-sided gorge or ravine using as many different methods as possible: walking, swimming, abseiling (rappelling) beside or down the middle of waterfalls, jumping off high ledges, sliding down chutes. It's all about fun, adventure and exploration and it's bound to appeal strongly to the child in all of us. It requires a high level of commitment to participation and some jumps and abseils can be positively scary.

Canyoning as a sport rather than simply a method of exploration is a relatively recent innovation, developing in the last few decades. These days it's a highly specialised sport on which entire villages in France and Spain rely for summer income. There are commercial canyoning ventures all over the world, from Brazil to the Dominican Republic, and from Madagascar to, in recent years, New Zealand.

The costs of taking a commercial canyoning trip in this country start at around $100, although if you go to a mountain guide rather than a canyoning company you may be able to get it for less. The demands of canyoning trips vary enormously. In general, New Zealand canyons are steeper than European canyons, but they range from low-key, fun adventures like the trip I took, to hard-out "advanced" canyons with high water flow, 400-metre waterfalls, long continuous abseils and huge jumps. There is truly something for everyone: the trick is finding the right trip for you. And the best way to do that is by asking lots of questions. How long is the walk in? How high are the abseils? Are they wet or dry abseils? Is there the option of being lowered instead of abseiling? How high are the jumps? Is it possible to opt out of the higher jumps? How big are the slides?

One good clue to the nature of the trip is how old you have to be to go – if they only take adults it may be fairly demanding. If you're doing one of the gentler trips you won't need to be terrifically fit but you will need to be agile and not have any major health problems.

Back to the subject of safety: while world-wide there have been a large number of deaths while canyoning, there have been no deaths and only a very few minor injuries on commercial canyoning trips in New Zealand. The disaster at Interlaken, Switzerland, in 1999 that claimed the lives of 21 canyoners is unlikely to be repeated here: we don't get the same thunderstorms, and as long as the canyons are kept clear of debris flash-flooding should not occur.

Canyoning guides the world over are, understandably, now more careful than ever about monitoring weather conditions and riverflow. Some New Zealand guides have overseas canyoning qualifications, although a qualified mountain guide would have the skills to lead a canyoning trip.

Hypothermia and falls are the main dangers of canyoning in New Zealand. Hypothermia shouldn't be a problem with a decent wetsuit, but avoiding the falls is entirely up to you. Listen carefully to your guide, don't rush, be careful of slippery rocks – and have fun!

Questions to ask

1. What qualifications, training and experience do your guides have?
2. What is the ratio of guides to clients?
3. Do you supply shoes or booties or will I have to use my own shoes?
4. In the abseiling do I control my own descent or will I be lowered?
5. Can I bring my camera?

GORGE YOURSELF

You know that things aren't going to be all that tough when there's an eight-year-old along for the ride. This is surely an omen that the experience is going to be about fun not terror.

The nine of us – seven clients and two Twelve Mile Delta Canyoning guides – arrive at Twelve Mile Creek in the heat of the day and by the time we've struggled into our two-piece wetsuits, neoprene socks, booties, helmets, life jackets and nappy-like harnesses we're certainly feeling over-dressed.

We begin with a short walk, complete with nature talk and the inevitable corny jokes. When we get to the start we discover the first challenge is getting into the canyon itself. The creek is 30 metres below us at the bottom of a sheer cliff. To get there we'll have to be lowered one by one on a rope by our guides. It's a bit like abseiling but the guides have control instead of the clients. It's an act of faith to step out backwards over a 30-metre drop when the only thing between you and certain death is a man you've only just met and haven't had a chance to get a psychiatric report on. Still, we all manage it just fine, right down to the eight-year-old.

Well, we're there. We're in the canyon and there's only one way to go – downstream. We begin with a bit of a walk over the smooth, slippery rocks in the knee-deep creek. At 6°C the water is icily cold; it's fed by the glacial Lake Isobel high on the slopes of Mt Crichton. When we come to a short section of rapids we change our approach. We lie on our stomachs and launch ourselves into a head-first slide, hands in front of our faces, taking advantage of the padding provided by our wetsuits and bulky life jackets. It's a rough, slightly scary, ride – though it's not exactly painful it's fairly jarring on the old joints. But it's fun, and a taste of things to come. However we get down this creek, it's not going to be the easy way.

Shaded by bush high above us we continue through the sheer-walled canyon between water-scoured logs and smooth boulders. I imagine I'm one of the gold miners that worked rivers in the area, exploring the gorge looking for flakes or nuggets of gold in the black iron-sand.

There's something new around every corner: one minute we're walking like gorillas, the next we're sliding, then being lowered on the rope. Before long comes a more challenging proposition: a bum-slide down a steep, smooth 2.5-metre chute that becomes a 3-metre freefall into a pool. The prospect is all the more daunting because it's done blind – there's no way to see what's coming before you launch yourself down the waterfall. But launch I do, and it's a hell of a shock to feel the polished chute disappear from beneath me as I hurtle off the end and fall into the foaming pool. But, hey, it's fun . . .

The pool, nicknamed "The Room", is a watery playground with ample opportunities for swimming, leaping and diving under the pounding waterfall. The kids, and most of the big kids, love it, but I spend most of the time standing in a rare sunny spot trying to warm up my very chilly bones. Eventually we continue through "The Sperm Run", another face-first slide, this time through a magical gorge, very narrow with spectacularly steep walls.

The next pool offers all sorts of options for jumps from different heights, from a couple of metres and up. What makes these jumps really interesting is the precision required: the water is deep enough for jumping in only a very small area. "Oscar" – it's not really his name, but that's what's written on his helmet – shows us exactly where to hit the water, bomb-style. I don't feel sure I can be that accurate and all around are rocks and sand banks. What if I misjudge it? What if I slip on take-off?

I take a deep, steadying breath, then make a careful leap. Bang! I hit the water hard before bottoming out on the sandy bed. Oscar says I'm the best jumper of the group – but I think that just means I make the biggest splash.

There's not much further to go – a bit of walking, swimming and sliding, then one last, tricky "abseil" down an overhanging rock. A short walk back to the bus and we're stripping off our wetsuits and sitting in the sun to warm up, munching a barbecued sausage in bread and congratulating ourselves on meeting all the challenges of the Twelve Mile Creek.

It's been a fun day, a play day. We're all smiling.

→ Twelve Mile Delta Canyoning, Queenstown.
Freephone 0800 2 CANYON (0800 222 696).

JETBOATING

Huka Jet

New Zealand is the home of the jetboat, a high-power, made-for-thrills river boat. It was developed by local man Bill Hamilton in the 1950s and what makes it special is its manoeuvrability at high speed as well as its ability to navigate shallow rivers and travel rapids upstream. Jetboats get their ultra-high performance from powerful engines, flat hulls and revolutionary internal marine jet propulsion.

From the very beginning jetboats were used both for pleasure trips and as workhorses servicing the high-country farms of the South Island. Tourist jetboating started in earnest in 1970 when the new owner of the now-famous Shotover Jet, the rather appropriately named Trevor Gamble, discovered that he could give sightseers a bit of a rush by driving very close to the rock walls of the Shotover canyon. It wasn't until 1976, though, when he employed three young male drivers, that macho competitiveness raised the standard of driving and brought about the heart-pumping action that characterises modern jetboating.

Today there are commercial jetboating companies all over the country offering a range of trips. Many of them are low-key operators offering scenic tours or ferry services, and because they do not offer a high-adrenalin experience they are not included in this book. Of the operators that concentrate on action and excitement, some navigate rocky canyons and some tackle serious rapids, but most take advantage of the jetboat's ability to operate in as little as 10 centimetres of water to skim through shallow, braided rivers at anything up to 70 kph.

No jetboat trip would be complete without the famous Hamilton Spin. At least that's what most people call it – some companies like to rename it after themselves, for example, the Shotover Spin or the Longridge Jet Spin. Whatever you like to call it, this trademark manoeuvre sends the jetboat into a high speed, high G-force 360° spin in the space of a single boat length. It's always a crowd-pleaser.

Commercial jetboats are custom-built for the conditions in which they will be used. Generally the hulls are made from heavy-duty marine aluminium, and the boats powered by environmentally friendly liquid petroleum gas V8 engines driving New Zealand's own Hamilton Jet propulsion unit. They can carry anything from five to 15 passengers.

Jetboating is not entirely safe, but then no adventure tourism activity is. There have been fatal collisions, but with passenger numbers running into the millions the chances of being involved in an accident are absolutely tiny. The New Zealand Commercial Jetboat Association oversees a code of practice, and both operators and drivers must satisfy Marine Safety Authority regulations. Driver training has generally become much more exhaustive, and in Queenstown drivers have stopped swerving quite so close to rock walls as they used to – although it's still close enough to make the punters gasp.

Costs range from $10 to $100. Some operators, particularly those in tourist centres like Queenstown, have regular departures, but most work on an on-demand basis: you demand a trip and they'll supply it if they have enough passengers to make it worthwhile. Jetboating isn't strongly weather-dependent. If it's raining a bit you'll be supplied with a waterproof jacket, but if the weather is vile or the river is flooded you may find the trip is cancelled.

Small children are welcomed by most jetboat companies, and there is certainly no upper age limit. You should let the operator know if you're pregnant, have a neurological or heart condition, or a neck or back injury. Take with you warm clothing and sunglasses, and the operator will (or should) provide you with a spray jacket if necessary. They will definitely supply a life jacket.

Then just settle in and enjoy the ride.

ACCELERATED EXHILARATION

In winter and spring, when the unsealed road is turned to porridge by rain and snowmelt, the four-wheel-drive trip to the Skippers Canyon jetboat wharf is even more thrilling than the jetboat ride itself. And it's quite thrilling enough on a summer's day with the road baked hard.

Colin, our driver, is a rare bird – an older man working in the adventure tourism industry – and he handles the Land Rover with all the aplomb that decades of experience confer. He manages to give a full commentary as he rocks the vehicle up and down the Skippers Road, a historic gold-miners' route that has the distinction of being one of only a few public roads that rental car companies won't allow their cars to be taken on. He does, I'm glad to say, pause his commentary while taking particularly tricky unguarded corners cut into precipices. Helicopters dart past us up the valley, completing the journey in just a few minutes, while rafting buses towing trailers manoeuvre delicately past each other on the one-track road.

The sketchy road, which is subject to slips, winds through a rugged but magnificent canyon. The road was carved by hand from the rocks to service the many thousands of miners that swarmed the canyon after the first gold was found in 1862, but by the time it was finished, 20 years after work began, it was too late: most of the miners had moved on.

Down at the Upper Shotover River, our jetboat awaits us at the wharf. We put on life jackets and get in the boat and, after the briefest of technical talks – "Hold on!" – we're swishing and fish-tailing our way upstream. Our jetboat driver Ronnie is, like Colin, a descendant of gold-miners, and every now and then we stop to hear about the history of gold-mining on the river and to check out various abandoned sluices and dredges. The ride is pretty tame, but the odd swerve towards the rocky canyon walls is enough to keep us clutching the hand rails.

Under the Pipeline Bridge we pause to watch a bungy jumper 102 metres above us chicken out of the leap, before we continue our snaking route up the shallow river to the Skippers Bridge. It's turn-around time, and this is where the real fun begins. It's hell-for-leather back downstream, skimming the gravel banks at high speed, dodging the canyon walls at the very last moment, skirting rusted machinery, careening towards rocks only to veer away with a split second to spare. It's stomach-churning stuff, but we feel safe in the hands of our experienced driver – he's a family man not some wild-eyed, live-fast-die-young type. We never come closer to the canyon walls than about 2 metres, but at times it feels like we're a hair's breadth from instant death.

Ronnie also indulges in three Hamilton Spins: lock on and throttle off, then the nose dips hard and we're spinning on a sixpence with spray flying everywhere. Each time we're thrown forward or sideways or both: this is where the injunction to "Hold on!" is really important. Then in a fraction of the time it took us to do the upstream leg, we're back at the wharf.

We continue the tour by going by road to the Pipeline – and are offered the opportunity to do a bungy jump or ride the flying fox that spans the canyon parallel to the bridge. There's time for a cup of tea and a biscuit, a look around Winky's Museum of gold-mining artefacts, and a chance to pan for gold.

The Skippers Canyon Jet is a "value-added" jetboat experience: it takes up half a day, but you get much more than you do on the average jetboat trip. The road trip is spectacular, the history is stunning and the jetboat ride is thrilling.

→ Skippers Canyon Jet, Queenstown.
Freephone 0800 286 491.

JET-SPRINTING

Another New Zealand invention, the sport of jet-sprint was the bright idea of Margaret Quinn. In 1983 it occurred to her that jetboat racing would be much more spectator-friendly if the jetboats whizzed around a small, shallow, winding circuit rather than up a river. The Jetboat Association agreed and organised a race, and jet-sprinting was an instant hit. Soon jetboat clubs all over the country were running competitions for specially constructed jet-sprint boats, the formula one cars of the boating world.

Jet-sprinting is now available to all through a number of tourist ventures. At a couple of places paying passengers are taken around twisty purpose-built courses by experienced drivers in boats that can go from 0 to 50 kph in a couple of seconds, while at others you can drive yourself. Either way these under-sized, over-powered boats come equipped with features like a roll bar and full harness, and they have a pretty good safety record – although they haven't been around all that long.

The experience is quite different from jetboating. It's short, sweet and all action. From start to finish the G forces thrust you deep into your bucket seat or fling you from side to side (don't even think about going jet-sprinting if you have a neck injury). This isn't a scenic trip – the constant high-speed, hair's-breadth turns leave no time to look at the view – but you won't care because you'll be too busy bracing yourself for the crash that never comes.

WHITEWATER RAFTING

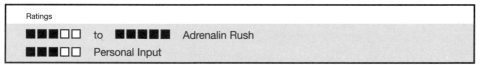

The whitewater raft – paddles flashing, spray flying – is one of the icons of the New Zealand adventure experience. This country is justly famous for its stunning mountain landscapes and untamed wilderness, and what more intense way is there to experience them than from an inflatable raft on a wild, fast-flowing river?

The whitewater rafters were amongst New Zealand's adventure tourism pioneers. Rafting took off in this country when cheap military surplus inflatable rafts came on to the market after World War II. By the 1960s the rafts were mostly worn out and replacements were expensive so the hard-core rafters got into a no-frills version of rafting involving truck inner tubes.

In the 1970s new materials lowered the price of inflatable rafts and there was an upsurge in the popularity of the sport in New Zealand. By the late 1970s one or two entrepreneurs had seen the tourism potential and within a few years there were more than 50 commercial rafting companies. These days commercial rafting companies all around New Zealand offer trips down rapids and through crashing whitewater. In the most popular areas – the central North Island around Rotorua and Taupo, the South Island's Buller region and Queenstown – there may be a number of competing operators running the same stretch of water. Prices start at around $65 for a short trip and can go as high as $350 for a full-day heli-rafting trip.

New Zealand rivers are small by world rafting standards – the rapids are a result of the gradient rather than a high volume of water. They're pool-drop rivers, which means that rafters get a chance to catch their breath in calm water between rapids and waterfalls. Both the central North Island and the Buller region have a great range of rivers of varying grades, so you're bound to find something to suit your temperament (for more about gradings see p. 54). Queenstown has fewer options, but it does have the world-famous – or infamous – Shotover River.

The large oar rafts so common overseas (remember Meryl Streep in *The River Wild*?) are not often used on our narrow rivers, partly because there's less room to swing the oars and partly because it's much more fun for the passengers if they help control the raft by paddling. The great thing is that as long as there's an experienced guide on board (and some companies use two in each boat), the only qualification you need to paddle even the biggest water is knowing the difference between left and right, and forwards and backwards.

Whitewater rafting is not completely safe. Indeed, the potential for disaster is one of the things that draws people to the sport. The fact is, though, that while they like to think they're doing a dangerous and daring activity they don't actually want to be the one to get hurt, and following a cluster of tourist drownings in the mid-1990s more stringent standards were developed in an attempt to make rafting as safe as an extreme sport in an extreme environment can be.

Rafting companies operate under a compulsory Marine Safety Authority code of practice and guides qualify under the New Zealand Rafting Association's award scheme – in Queenstown they have to meet the local council's regulations too. There is now a much greater emphasis on safety, more time is spent on off-river training, and operators won't take you out if river conditions are dangerous.

Nearly all rafting companies operate year-round, riverflow permitting, though I have to say I wouldn't be all that keen on risking a dunking in an icy alpine river in the middle of winter. A lot of companies have a minimum age of 13 for passengers but some will take kids as young as 10 on lower-grade rivers. As with all water activities you'll need to fit the gear – wetsuits, life jackets, etc. – but that should only be a problem if you are extremely heavy.

Rafting can be a fairly vigorous activity, especially in big water, so a reasonable level of fitness is an advantage. Water confidence is a must and I'd suggest that if you're tackling a grade 4 or 5 river you should be a good swimmer. Make sure you inform the operator if you have any serious medical conditions. If you appear to be under the influence of drugs or alcohol you won't be allowed on the raft – and you may not even get your money back.

Despite the inherent dangers – or perhaps because of them – whitewater rafting is one of the most thrilling and rewarding outdoor activities available in New Zealand. It's a must-do for anyone seeking the adventurer within.

RAPID DESCENT

The Kaituna Cascades rafting guides are called Graz and Eric: Graz is a stereotypically laid-back New Zealander, Eric a lively American. Graz is going to be at the back steering – he's the boss – and Eric at the front doing the hard work as they take us through one of the most intense whitewater rafting trips in the world. The highlight of the Okere Falls run on the Kaituna River is (take a deep breath) the world's highest commercially rafted waterfall.

At the riverside base north of Lake Rotorua we change into swimsuits or shorts, a groovy animal-print fleece top, life jacket, helmet and booties. There's no need to wear a wetsuit: it's February and the water temperature is 20°C. The fleece is more to keep the sun off than anything.

On dry land Eric sits the four of us punters in our allotted positions in the inflatable raft and we learn the drill: backwards and forwards strokes, grabbing a rope for serious rapids, and the all-important "Hold on!" position for the three waterfalls. We learn to jam ourselves in on the floor of the raft and grab for a rope with each hand, all the while trying not to bean anyone with the paddle. We practise this a lot. We also learn what to do if the boat flips. At this point I switch off – I don't want to think about this possibility.

We go through these drills a number of times: again with Graz at the base, once more with Eric at the water's edge, and a couple of times on calm water. It's tediously repetitive but I'm about to discover why it's important to burn it into your mind.

Then we're off down into a steep, narrow canyon cut through volcanic rock by the raging river: bouncing through a little rapid or two, then over our first small waterfall. We all get down in time at the call of "Hold on!" and go crashing over the fall. We've passed our first test, although I'm a bit worried by the paddling team's lack of co-ordination and clashing of paddles.

We continue through the run's 14 drops, going through rapids forwards, backwards and spinning, honing our skills and building our confidence. Before we reach the 7-metre Tutea Falls (yes, that's just about the height of a two-storey building) we pause for a last pep talk. Then we're paddling hard towards the roaring waterfall while Graz lines us up. There's no going back. At the very last minute, "Hold on!" sends us scrambling to the floor and then we're dropping down nose-first, down, down, then we hit – and flip.

I'm under water and it's like a washing machine. I'm hanging on because I've been told to hang on, but the raft is above me and I'm running out of air and my body tells me I could die if I stay down here. I let go and wait to pop up to the surface but I'm tumbling and turning and staying under – then I'm up and gulping air. The raft is miles away and I swim towards it but I don't seem to be making any progress because the current is pulling me downstream. I don't want to go through the next rapid on my own so I give my paddle to Graz and swim harder and before long I'm being pulled into the raft and we're all there and we're all alive.

After that it seems easy. We go over a few more rapids, drop over the side of the raft for a quick swim, and surf the churning water at the base of a rapid while water cascades into the self-bailing raft. We're a smooth, professional team, such experts that we even go down one rapid standing up.

And then it's all over. I have laughed in the face of danger on a clear river in a stunningly beautiful canyon and as I'm driving home round the top of Lake Rotorua the world seems a wonderful place, more beautiful than ever before, and it's a privilege to be alive.

It's only that night, as I struggle to relax into sleep, that the significance of the day hits me. When the raft flipped I probably wasn't under water all that long – maybe five seconds, eight tops – but it seemed like eternity, and for the first time in my life I felt that I might die right here, right now. It's a disturbing thought.

→ Kaituna Cascades, Rotorua.
  Freephone 0800 KAITUNA (0800 524 886).

WHITEWATER KAYAKING

Ratings	
■■■□□	Adrenalin Rush
■■■■■	Personal Input

Kayaks are considered the elite of the river-running craft: they're more versatile, more manoeuvrable and more fun than rafts. If you wanted to take on New Zealand's really big whitewater – the "nearly impossible" grade 6 rapids – you'd probably take a kayak. But first you'd take a lot of lessons (not to mention a psychiatric test) because kayaks take a good deal of skill to paddle in whitewater.

These small, closed, keelless boats, sometimes called canoes, were developed over thousands of years by the native peoples of Arctic North America and Greenland for use in fishing and hunting. The original kayaks were built by stretching animal skins over driftwood or whalebone frames and were able to be righted without taking on water, hence the "Eskimo roll".

It was a Scotsman, John MacGregor, who in the 1860s was responsible for recreational kayaking in the form we know it today. He adapted the native designs and built decked kayaks that had sails as well as paddles, and he founded the Canoe Club. The kayaking craze, the craze that would lead to the sleek, high-tech river and sea kayaks of today, had begun.

Whitewater kayaking is the sort of sport where the better you are, the more fun you have. You shouldn't expect to master kayaking in a day. With good instruction from a New Zealand Outdoor Instructors Association kayak guide or someone with equivalent teaching experience, a carefully selected river and the right type of kayak you won't be ready to hit the grade 6 water – but you should be able to tackle grade 2 rapids, maybe even grade 3, with confidence, do impressive eddy turns, and surf standing waves. (For more information on river grades see p. 54.)

A beginner's whitewater kayaking day is an intense learning experience. The kayak is an inherently unstable craft, and you need to use a number of different techniques to (try to) control it. You'll need to be fit and to be able to swim confidently because sooner or later you're going to end up in the drink, and any sort of serious medical condition or disability will present a problem. Kayakers can't be too big: the cockpit is quite small and it's a tight fit for larger people. Children as young as 10 can learn whitewater kayaking, as long as they're reasonably mature.

Whitewater kayaking is, by definition, not a gentle paddle down a placid river. Running wild water is a draining experience whether you do it with a raft, river board, sledge or kayak. It's just plain scary. But remember that, although the sport of whitewater kayaking as a whole doesn't have a great safety record, it's highly unlikely you'll come a serious cropper on a grade 2 river.

What makes whitewater kayaking so rewarding is that at the end of a day on the river you can say you ran the rapids on your own, that you weren't just a passenger . . . that, to be utterly corny, you paddled your own canoe.

Questions to ask

1. What type of kayaks do you use?
2. Is there a sustained level of difficulty or are there long stretches of easy water?
3. What ratio of instructors to clients will there be?
4. Do you supply all the gear and clothing I'll need?
5. What do you supply in the way of food?
6. Do you have hot showers?

INFLATABLE KAYAKS

Inflatable kayaks, of which Funyaks are one type, are really small, kayak-shaped inflatable rafts. Just like an ordinary kayak, you sit inside and use a double-bladed paddle. They're ideal for beginner kayakers because they're safe and very forgiving. Although they're not very manoeuvrable, they are extremely stable, and new paddlers don't have to learn drills for wet exits or master eddy turns as they would have to in an ordinary kayak.

In an inflatable kayak a fast-learning beginner can expect to be able to conquer grade 3 rapids – quite a thrill for your first day.

CATCHING WAVES

We'll be kayaking the Clutha River, the Alpine River Guides instructor tells us. The Clutha River? The mighty Clutha, the massive river that thunders through the Clyde Dam? I don't *think* so, not me. Don't worry, Alan says, we'll be paddling the river close to its source, Lake Wanaka. It's running low – only 164,000 litres per second, less than one-tenth of the 1999 peak. Still sounds a lot to me.

When we arrive at the river it doesn't look so bad – it's wide and fast-flowing but reassuringly flat. We get kitted out: polypropylene thermal top, sleeveless wetsuit, booties, paddle jacket, life jacket, baseball cap, helmet and spray deck around the waist. In colder weather extra polyprops are on offer, as well as a balaclava for added glamour.

We settle down on the riverbank and Alan teaches us the basics. My stomach knots as I try to imagine using the strokes and stabilising techniques in grade 2 rapids – it's one thing to be sitting in a kayak on dry land, quite another to be running rapids with waves up to a metre high. Then we go to a flat section of the river to try out our skills and gain confidence.

For the rest of the morning we practise, practise and practise again. We learn how to get from one side of the river to the other (harder than you might think), how to break out of the still water of an eddy into the fast-moving current and how to break back in again, and how to stabilise ourselves as we lean into turns. We're cramming a couple of days' worth of instruction into a couple of hours and we need to learn fast.

It starts to sink in that we're in for some serious paddling when Alan takes us to a deep, clear pool to teach us what to do if – when – we capsize. We go through the routine: reach forward to release the spray deck (it forms a watertight seal over the cockpit), move the hands around to the side to remove the deck, and push out. Then we actually have to do it, more than anything to prove to ourselves that it can be done.

After a couple of nervy false starts I deliberately capsize my kayak – then panic. I fumble around in the dark trying to find the tag that releases the deck, then push, squirm and twist my way out. It probably takes about five seconds but it seems like a lifetime. Alan helpfully points out that if I open my eyes I might find it easier. Now why didn't I think of that? I try it again and this time I am calm, composed and efficient.

After a picnic lunch by the side of the river, we set off down the pure, clear, greeny-blue river to our first set of rapids. From this close to the action the very minor Deans Rapid looks like boiling, raging whitewater. I try to concentrate on Alan's earlier instructions: follow his line, keep the kayak straight, keep the hips loose. As the kayak bobs around on the surface like a cork, skewing to left and right, tipping over dangerously, I anxiously await the inevitable

TANDEM KAYAKS

If you want to go straight to a grade 5 extreme kayaking experience without needing to learn the finer points of kayaking there are a couple of operators who can organise it for you. For your introduction to big water you'll take the front seat of a Topolino tandem kayak and an experienced kayaking guide will take the back seat. The guide will take you over waterfalls and through major rapids, picking the lines and Eskimo-rolling the kayak if you capsize. You might be only a passenger, but it's a great ride.

capsize . . . and it doesn't come. I've made it through my first rapids!

We continue down the river, relaxing and drifting through the flat sections while Alan points out landmarks: historic Albert Town, the impressive Hallidays Bluff, a massive hole in the riverbank scoured by the floods of 1999, a gold stamping battery.

After a while we can predict when we're about to get to a difficult bit – we always stop for a sweetie. The rapids seem to be getting harder, although our paddling is getting better too. There are lots of moments of anxiety, even fear: at one point panic strikes as I plough straight towards a wave nigh on a metre high – then go up it and through it as water crashes all over me.

I'm busy congratulating myself on successfully negotiating the Snake Point Rapids when, attempting a particularly stylish break-out, I unexpectedly find myself upside-down. My first reaction is bewilderment: what the hell am I doing here? This is quickly replaced by a sense of impotent acceptance then, fortunately, a feeling of urgency: I'd better get out of here! I run through the drill and seconds later I'm out and bobbing down the river with the end of my kayak in one hand and the paddle in the other. Strangely enough, the capsize doesn't destroy my confidence – it reinforces it. I can push things harder now that I know that I can get safely out of the kayak if I need to.

Below one small set of rocky rapids we pause while Alan teaches us how to surf a standing wave. When my turn comes I paddle my way upstream to a rock and find that, illogically, when I stop paddling the kayak stays put. I'm surfing the recirculating water, and it's a real buzz. With delicate steering strokes to keep the kayak straight I can stay there as long as I want to.

At the end of a long day that has passed more quickly than any of us could have imagined, we take the kayaks out of the water at Luggate. We've navigated 22 kilometres of the Clutha River and survived four decent rapids. All of us have capsized at least once – except for a stiff, anxious Englishman called Giles who obviously wasn't trying hard enough. Over hot drinks and home-made muffins everyone is glowing with pleasure, even the Canadian doctor who claims the only time she has experienced stress like this was when a patient dropped dead in her office.

→ Alpine River Guides, Wanaka.
Phone 0-3-443 9023.

WHITEWATER SLEDGING & RIVER BOARDING

Ratings	
■■■□□	Adrenalin Rush
■■■■■	Personal Input

Serious Fun River Surfing

If whitewater kayaking is too tame for you, and whitewater rafting is old hat, then it's time to throw away the paddle, hop out of the boat and get in amongst it. The two distinct sports of whitewater sledging and river boarding are variations on a theme: both give you the chance to get up close and personal with New Zealand's raging whitewater.

Whitewater sledging has been around since 1981 in France (where it is known as hydrospeed) but it took a few more years for the sport to make it to New Zealand. The idea is that you rest the top half of your body on a sledge – it comes complete with handles and arm rests – and manoeuvre your way down the river by kicking with fins. The sledge provides buoyancy and protects your body like a shield.

River boarding works in much the same way as sledging but with different gear. It all began with a Hawaiian backpacker called Jon Imhoof who in 1989 started taking tourists on free trips down the Kawarau River rapids on bodyboards (aka boogie boards); a year later he started Serious Fun, the first commercial river boarding operation in the world. You ride the modified bodyboard the same way you would in the sea, with your hands holding the edge at the front and your forearms resting on the board.

There is a certain friendly rivalry between operators over which is better: sledging or boarding. The sledging companies claim their guides have more exhaustive training (overseen by the New Zealand Whitewater Sledging Association) and point out that sledges are specially designed for river use. River boarding nuts say that their boards are more manoeuvrable and you can do more tricks on them. The consensus is that while both sports offer a wild ride, river boarding is just a little more extreme.

To get the best out of both versions you need a high-volume pool-drop river because this type of river doesn't have lots of exposed rock either in the rapids or the pools below. This type of river also has safe places to stop and play: small "whirlies" to ride and standing waves on which to surf. In high-volume rivers there's less chance of hitting or getting pinned against rocks or submerged debris, and so far as I'm aware there haven't been any fatalities on river boarding or sledging trips in this country, and only a very few injuries.

Operators are keen to differentiate themselves: a Hawera trip includes a 5-metre slide down a weir, one Queenstown operator can tow you with a jetski, another gives you longer in the water. It's worth doing a bit of research to find the best trip for you. Some companies offer trips of varying difficulty on different rivers: everything from grade 1 to grade 5 (for more information about the grades and what they mean, see p. 54). Trips cost from $75 to $110 or more.

If you choose a trip that includes serious whitewater, you'll need to be fit, and a strong and confident swimmer. Young children probably won't enjoy the more severe rapids, although most companies will take kids under 15 if, after consultation with the parents, they think they're up to it. Size doesn't have to be a problem, so long as you can fit the wetsuit and life jacket. If you're pregnant or have any serious medical condition you'll need to discuss this with the operator before booking the trip.

The most important quality for anyone taking one of these trips is a good attitude. It's not like rafting or jetboating, where the guides are in control and you are just a passenger. In river boarding and sledging you are in charge – as one operator puts it, you are the master of your own destiny. Although there are experienced guides in the water with you, there is only so much they can do to help you stay out of trouble. It's up to you to concentrate and to follow instructions carefully – but it's you who'll get the kudos at the end.

Questions to ask

1. What is the best river for my level of fitness, confidence and ability?
2. What ratio of guides to clients will there be on the trip?
3. Are there places I can get out of the river if I find the going too hard?
4. What's the scenery like?

RIVER BUGS

River bugging is the latest addition to the repertoire of New Zealand's whitewater operators. Yet another Kiwi adventure invention, the river bug is a single-person raft with inflatable buoyancy chambers behind, beneath and beside the, um, bugger. These ensure you stay on top of the water, while extra-thick padding turns colliding with rocks into a low-impact dodgems ride.

You'll be kitted out in padded wetsuit, helmet, life jacket, booties, fins and special webbed gloves for paddling. You sit in the raft with your feet hanging in the water – in fact it's more like an easy chair than a raft. After learning a few basic skills you're ready to run the rapids, catch eddies, surf standing waves and pirouette.

You don't need to be very fit to go river bugging, but you can't weigh more than about 100 kg. As always, medical conditions should be reported to the operator.

ALIVE AND KICKING (HARD)

It starts off pretty cruisy – a ride in a bus with just a small group of four punters. Our young guides, Scotty and Becks, with their tans and sun-bleached hair would both fit in happily on a surf beach. Becks is one of a relatively select group of female whitewater guides, and is the only woman river boarding guide in the area.

At the roadside we put on our wetsuits, booties, life jackets and helmets, pick up our boogie boards and head down to the Kawarau River at the Roaring Meg rapids. A few minutes later, having been given our instructions on technique and safety, we pull on our fins and we're off down the grade 3 rapids.

It's a pretty simple sport really. Just point your board in the direction you want to go and kick. It's no good fighting the current: with a high-volume, fast-moving river like the Kawarau it's going to be a losing battle. The problem is that when you hop in the water for the first time you're not quite sure of the best way to make friends with it.

After a few minutes of kicking my way through, over, under, around and across eddies, whirlpools and rapids with metre-high waves, I'm knackered. My leg muscles are burning and I'm gasping for air – and as often as not breathing in water. This is whitewater rafting from an entirely different angle, with your face in the rapids instead of a paddle.

Don't get me wrong . . . I *am* having fun. I just don't know it yet. River boarding in grade 3 or 4 rapids is a full-on, go-hard experience that involves, in my case, a little fear. There's no getting away from it: whitewater rivers are dangerous places and, although I know this section of the Kawarau is reasonably safe because it is very deep and so doesn't have hidden logs or rocks to trap me, this information is not getting through to my adrenal glands. River boarding is exhilarating, challenging and exciting – what more could you ask for in an extreme sport? – but it sure as hell ain't for wimps.

And it looks like I'm in danger of becoming a wimp. The relentlessness of it all is starting to get to me, rapids upon foaming rapids with few chances to catch my breath and relax. The things I hoped to do, the tricks that make river boarding unique, seem impossible when it's all I can do to keep things together. "Squirting", in which you and your board travel underwater for up to 10 seconds, and surfing a standing wave just aren't options for me.

Things improve as I go, however, and by the end of the run I've learnt a few things: that if you relax and take things easy in the smoother sections you'll have more energy for the rapids; that there's no need to panic if you get ahead of both guides (don't worry, they always know where you are); that it's easier to go with the current than across it; and that life is a lot more pleasant in the middle of the river than banging against the rocks at the edges.

By the time we finish the run, I'm starting to get the hang of it, starting to feel more in control, starting to think I could really enjoy this. Running the rapids is getting to be thrilling rather than terrifying. The problem is, I'm tired. Really tired. Maybe I'm not quite the girl-jock adventurer I thought I was – or maybe it has something to do with consuming nothing but a bowl of cereal and a muesli bar (oh, and half a pint of nutritious beer) in the last 24 hours.

So, although when we're offered a second run down the same section of river I'm keen to give it a go, I opt out, preferring to soak up the sun and wait for the others. In no time at all, it seems, they've completed the second run. They're honking with excitement – this time, they say, it was much easier, more relaxed, much more fun. They knew what they were doing and they knew what was coming. They even managed to get three of them all surfing upstream on the same standing wave.

I try not to be jealous, try to convince myself I made the right decision. There's only one thing for it – I'll have to go back one day and do it again.

→ Serious Fun River Surfing, Queenstown.
   Freephone 0800 737 468.

SWIMMING WITH DOLPHINS

Ratings	
■■□□□	Adrenalin Rush
■■□□□	Personal Input

What does swimming with dolphins mean to you? Frolicking for hours with friendly, trusting creatures, stroking their smooth skins, playing games with them, perhaps even going for rides on their backs, clutching a flipper to keep your balance? If it does you've watched too many episodes of *Flipper* and forgotten that dolphins are wild animals, free to come and go as they please. It is a privilege to be in the company of these astonishingly beautiful and intelligent creatures, but they are not pets and they have no particular reason to hang around human beings, let alone entertain them.

If you want to be guaranteed a close-quarters experience you'll need to go to one of the theme parks and research centres around the world that allow you to swim with dolphins in pools or netted areas – in fact you can do this in New Zealand, at Napier's Marineland – but these dolphins are likely to be tired and bored after years of doing tricks. Most people who are in love with the idea of dolphins crave an encounter with *wild* dolphins, and numerous New Zealand operators – all controlled by Department of Conservation regulations – offer boat-based snorkelling trips to do just this.

Different people have very different experiences swimming with dolphins in New Zealand. While on some trips pods of hundreds of dolphins are quickly found and they are happy to spend time investigating the human intruders, even approaching and playing with them for extended periods, other swimmers are not so lucky. Sometimes it takes an age to find the dolphins (operators are not allowed to attract them with food), then they surf the vessel's bow wave for a while only to retreat not long after the swimmers get in the water.

There are a few tricks to getting the best from your dolphin experience. If you haven't snorkelled before, practise before you go: once you're in the water there's no time to waste fiddling with your mask. When you first find dolphins make the most of the viewing time that most operators offer before you start swimming. Go up to the bow where at very close quarters you can watch – and listen to – the dolphins surfing the bow wave. Have all your gear on, ready to get in the water when it's your turn and try to make sure that at least once during the trip you're the first from your group to get in.

Get into the water as quickly and quietly as you can, and once you're in put your mask straight in the water and keep looking down. If you can't see any dolphins don't take your face out of the water to look around because while you're doing that you may miss a dolphin swimming below you. If a dolphin does approach, remember that it is in charge. Dolphins may be curious but they're not reckless so they're unlikely to come closer than a couple of metres. Try to resist the temptation to try to touch or chase the dolphins: you may drive them away. Some dolphins seem to enjoy being serenaded, so try singing a few show tunes through your snorkel.

If you go out with one of the operators in the Bay of Islands, in the far north of the country, you can expect to see playful common dolphins and bottlenose dolphins. In the shallow waters of the Bay of Plenty you'll find common dolphins again, but not so many bottlenose dolphins. Kaikoura is recognised as the home of dolphin swimming in New Zealand and there huge pods of dusky dolphins, the acrobats of the dolphin world, are easily found in the summer months, and Hector's, common and bottlenose dolphins also put in an appearance. Off Lyttelton you'll likely

SWIMMING WITH SEALS

This interesting – and cheaper – variation on swimming with dolphins is available at Kaikoura and further north in Nelson and Marlborough. The New Zealand fur seal, a large and sometimes frightening creature when encountered on land, is a pussycat when it's in the water.

Some operators offer boat trips while others are shore-based – and both versions have their pluses. Boat trips allow the operator to vary the sites they use and stay away from areas where the seals have a lot of human interaction, while shore-based trips are less disruptive of the seals' natural environment. Both types of operation should supply you with a wetsuit and snorkelling equipment, and some have flotation aids for non-swimmers.

Don't forget that seals are wild animals: they're not there to entertain you. It is simply a privilege to spend some time with them in their home.

find the small, friendly but endangered Hector's dolphin, also known as the "downunder dolphin" because it is only found in New Zealand waters.

Commercial dolphin swimming outfits in this country offer trips costing from $70 to $95. There is a range of styles of operation, from charter fishing boats doing a sideline in dolphin swimming to purpose-built catamarans with air-conditioning, underwater cameras and special decks that enable easy entry into the water. All should supply wetsuits, masks, fins and snorkels, as well as flotation devices for people who are not confident swimmers.

Some operators will take children as young as six, as long as they are confident in the water, and most allow non-swimming passengers to come along at a reduced price if there's space. It's worth finding out how many swimmers there will be on board and how many groups you will be divided into: if there are lots of swimmers divided into two or three groups taking turns to go in, you will spend less time in the water. Medical conditions that might prevent you swimming with dolphins include pregnancy, heart conditions, back injuries, restricted mobility, asthma and epilepsy – but check with the operator.

Dolphin swimming is weather-dependent, so book to take the trip early in your stay. It's not a good idea to go out if the sea is rough because the dolphins are hard to spot, underwater visibility is poor – and there's more chance you'll get seasick. A good operator will cancel the trip if conditions aren't ideal. Early morning is a great time to go because the winds are usually lighter then. It's often cooler out at sea, so take warm outdoor clothes with you.

Swimming with dolphins – or seals for that matter – is not at the extreme end of the adventure tourism spectrum, and it certainly isn't a dangerous sport. However, it is a true adventure in the realm of the creatures of the sea, one that you will always remember.

Questions to ask

1. Will there be a marine studies expert on board to tell us about the marine wildlife?
2. How long does it usually take to find dolphins?
3. How many swimmers do you have in the water at one time?
4. How many groups will we be divided into?

BETWEEN THE DOLPHIN AND THE DEEP BLUE SEA

We arrive with high expectations. Perhaps too high. My friend Marion is fascinated by dolphins: one wall of her home is covered with posters of dolphins, she has books about dolphins, she has endless dolphin trinkets. Having swum with dolphins before, in a netted enclosure at Eilat in Israel, she feels she has a special bond with them. She is even half-jokingly hopeful that a dolphin may touch her sore back and heal her.

We're met at the Mt Maunganui wharf by down-to-earth Denny, the owner of Dolphin Seafaris, and Haydon, his enthusiastic crewman. We'll be a relatively small group: eight or nine swimmers plus a couple of others only interested in watching. Minutes later our boat, which doubles as a charter fishing boat, is heading out on calm seas into a sunny Bay of Plenty morning.

In the cockpit Haydon explains how to put on our wetsuits and fits us out with snorkelling gear, before chatting briefly about the history of the area and the wildlife we can expect to see. He divides us into two groups: we don't want to overwhelm the dolphins so we won't all be swimming at the same time.

The search begins. For a while we all eagerly scan the sparkling waters hoping to be the first to spot a dolphin, but as time wears on we start to lose enthusiasm and Marion and I start sunbathing instead. Denny is high up at the helm, binoculars glued to his eyes, on the lookout.

Just as, after an hour or more, we're starting to give up any hope of finding dolphins, Haydon lets out a yell. By the time we look out to sea, there are dozens of bottlenose dolphins streaking through the water beside us, making arcing leaps alone or in pairs. The excitement level moves up a few notches, then moves up a couple more when we discover that five or six of them are right under our noses, surfing the vibrant, clear-blue bow wave. Marion is buzzing. She has a sparkle in her eye and a wide smile: she is at last close to her dolphin friends.

Below us the huge mammals, 3 or 4 metres in length, jostle for space just under the surface, switching positions and communicating with each other with high-pitched squeaks. Every 10 or 15 seconds they come up for air, breaking the surface briefly and spraying us with water as they exhale sharply. One curious dolphin keeps turning onto its side so that it can get a good look at the peculiar creatures above. Further away from the boat another performs high, twisting leaps.

After 10 or 15 minutes of viewing and photography, the first group – my group – is sent into the water. Haydon encourages us to slip into the water as smoothly and quietly as possible, but it's hard to get down the ladder in fins. As soon as I look down I find there are a couple of dolphins below me. They check me out, then move on. I kick my way around to the front of the boat, keeping my face in the water as much as possible, and when I spot another dolphin I dive as deeply as I can. I have piqued the dolphin's curiosity and it swims rapidly towards me. My heart misses a beat – for a split second I think it might hit me – but at the last moment, when it's about a metre away, it veers to one side.

After 10 minutes or so Haydon, who has been swimming with us, calls us out of the water and sends the next group in. As we pull off our fins we breathlessly exchange notes about our encounters. Everyone has at least seen a dolphin, although only a few of us have got close. Some are very excited about finding themselves swimming not only with dolphins but also a pair of gentle pilot whales.

The second group comes back aboard when the last of the dolphins disappears, and Denny fires up the engine to go looking for more. For a time the whales accompany us on the search. When we come across the dolphins we immediately start swimming, with the other group going first this time. But the dolphins are losing interest and by the time I get in the water I catch only fleeting glimpses. Tantalisingly I can hear their squeaking all around but can't see them.

We move on and have one more dip, but the dolphins have scattered. The show – for them and for us – is over.

On the way back to the wharf Marion has a wistful look about her. She's thrilled but at the same time she's disappointed. I can understand why: even though we both knew before we started that there was a good chance the dolphins wouldn't stay around, we couldn't help hoping that maybe they'd see something special in us and want to play.

Still, Marion says, she has seen and spent time with her beloved dolphins. She's happy.

→ Dolphin Seafaris, Mt Maunganui.
Freephone 0800 ECOTRIP (0800 326 874).

SWIMMING WITH SHARKS

For something completely different, how about an adrenalin-pumping encounter with a shark? Yes, you can come face to face with a shark in its natural environment – without risking a ghastly death.

Since 1999 several boat operators have offered shark-diving trips in spring and summer. They lower a purpose-built, shark-proof metal cage from a boat out at sea, then lure sharks to the boat using fishy bait. You climb down into the cage and witness the underwater feeding frenzy while breathing through a regulator or snorkel (you, not the sharks). You can expect to see mako and/or blue sharks, both of which are aggressive, powerful creatures up to about 4 metres long. These graceful killers may well come close enough to touch – if you're dumb enough to put your hand outside the cage.

It's not an activity for young kids: you have to be at least 12 years old (and with one operator 15) to do it. You don't need to be able to swim but water confidence is a plus. No diving experience is required, but if you have any medical conditions check with the operator before going out – a number of conditions may be an issue when scuba diving.

If you're susceptible to motion sickness, it's a good idea to get preventative medication, because you may have to bob around at sea for some time while you wait for the sharks to arrive. You're less likely to have to wait in mid to late summer, when the sharks are around in the greatest numbers.

DIRECTORY 0

F OPERATORS

NORTH ISLAND

PAIHIA●

● WHANGAREI

DARGAVILLE ●

AUCKLAND ●

● PAUANUI BEACH

THAMES ●

NGARUAWAHIA ●
MATAMATA
HAMILTON ●
CAMBRIDGE ●

MT MAUNGANUI
● TAURANGA

TE PUKE
● WHAKATANE
● OPOTIKI

WAITOMO CAVES ●

ROTORUA ●

● TAUPO

NEW PLYMOUTH ●

NATIONAL ● TURANGI
PARK ●

● GISBORNE

TAIHAPE

NAPIER ●
HAVELOCK NORTH

HAWERA ●
WAITOTARA ●
WANGANUI ●
MANGAWEKA ●

WAIPUKURAU ●

PALMERSTON NORTH ●

PAEKAKARIKI ●

● MASTERTON

WELLINGTON ●

CARTERTON ●

KARAMEA
MOTUEKA
FRENCH PASS
NELSON
WESTPORT
MURCHISON
BLENHEIM
GREYMOUTH
HANMER SPRINGS
KAIKOURA
CHEVIOT
CASTLE HILL
FRANZ JOSEF
FOX GLACIER
SPRINGFIELD
CHRISTCHURCH
METHVEN
GERALDINE
ASHBURTON
AKAROA
TWIZEL
WANAKA
QUEENSTOWN
DUNEDIN

SOUTH ISLAND

OPERATORS

NORTH ISLAND

PAIHIA

TANDEM SKYDIVING

Sky-Hi Tandem Skydive

Phone 0-9-402 6744 Mobile phone 025 756 758 Fax 0-9-402 6745
Email sky-hi@xtra.co.nz Website home.xtra.co.nz/hosts/sky-hi/

Season	Year-round
Airfield	Paihia
Time to allow	1 hour
Bring with you	Comfortable outdoor clothing, sensible shoes, small camera
Cost	$185 (9000 ft)
Optional extras	Action photo, T-shirt
Operator's sales pitch	Experience the thrill of a tandem skydive in the awesome Bay of Islands, at the warmest drop zone in New Zealand.

ZORB

Zorb Northland Puketona Road, Haruru Falls, Paihia

Mobile phone 025 208 1319 Email zorbnorth@zorb.com Website www.zorb.com

Discounts	Group, family
Season	Year-round
Time to allow	8 minutes
Cost	$35
Operator's sales pitch	We are only 5 minutes from Paihia, the centre of the Bay of Islands. We operate on open farmland adjacent to the Watea airstrip, from which the Sky-Hi tandem skydivers go.
Other activities offered	Short Argo rides

DARGAVILLE

JETBOATING

Kaipara Kapers

Phone 0-9-431 7493 Mobile phone 025 239 9675 Fax 0-9-431 7493
Email kkjetboat@xtra.co.nz Website www.try.at/jetboat

Discounts	Group, family
Season	Year-round
Departures	Hourly and on demand
Launch site	Commercial wharf
Time to allow	Varies
Time on water	Varies: 15 minutes to 6 hours
Cost	From $10
Optional extras	Video, action photo
Operator's sales pitch	Our trips are really exciting, adrenalin pumping and safe. Longer trips that incorporate sand bikes and lunch are also available.
Other activities offered	Longer jetboat trips, sand quadbikes, "Bigfoot" bus beach trips

AUCKLAND

CANYONING

AWOL Canyoning Adventures

Phone 0-9-630 7100 Fax 0-9-623 0505
Email info@awoladventures.co.nz Website www.awoladventures.co.nz

Discounts	VIP, YHA, Kiwi Experience, Magic Bus, NZ Outside, group, family
Season	Year-round
Canyon	Piha valley
Time to allow	5–7 hours
Time in water	2.5–3.5 hours
Bring with you	Shoes for in water, towel, swimsuit
Cost	$125 (includes transport ex Auckland, bakery lunch, Piha surf beach visit)
Optional extras	Action photos, T-shirt
Operator's sales pitch	Start your experience over the 80-m Kitekite Falls, abseiling under waterfalls separated by tranquil pools. Jump and slide through this historic logging canyon. All caves and jumps are optional – choose the level of adventure!
Other activities offered	Abseiling (groups), team building

Canyonz

Phone 0-9-534 1468 Mobile phone 025 294 7724 Fax 0-9-534 1468
Email info@canyonz.co.nz Website www.canyonz.co.nz

Discounts	VIP, YHA, Kiwi Experience, Magic Bus, NZ Outside, group, family
Season	October–June
Canyon	Blue Canyon, Waitakere
Time to allow	8 hours
Time in water	3 hours minimum
Bring with you	Shoes for in water, towel, swimsuit, change of clothes
Cost	$135 (includes transport, food, Karekare beach visit)
Optional extras	Waterproof cameras, T-shirt
Operator's sales pitch	The Blue Canyon has countless jumps and slides, from mild to wild. Our clients learn to abseil waterfalls amidst spectacular native bush, and get 4 hours of actual canyoning.

HOT AIR BALLOONING

Balloon Expedition Co of New Zealand

Phone 0-9-416 8590 Mobile phone 021 995 501 Fax 0-9-416 8590 Email balexped@ihug.co.nz

Discounts	NZ Outside
Season	Year-round
Time to allow	4 hours
Flight time	1–1.5 hours
Bring with you	Warm outdoor clothing
Cost	$220 (includes transport, champagne breakfast)
Operator's sales pitch	We're the only operator to fly over Auckland city and the Waitemata Harbour (when wind direction/speed allow). Most flights end within 20 km of the centre of Auckland.
Other activities offered	Balloon tours throughout New Zealand

TANDEM HANG GLIDING

Aqua Air Adventure

Freephone 0508 GET HIGH (0508 438 4444) Mobile phone 021 644 543 Fax 0-9-528 7594
Email aqua@ihug.co.nz

Season	Year-round
Time to allow	2–3 hours
Flight time	2–3 minutes
Bring with you	Old clothing
Cost	$60
Optional extras	Action photo, T-shirt
Operator's sales pitch	You'll take off from flat ground, lying down beside the instructor, then be towed up to 650 ft by a quad bike. After release you'll be shown how to fly and can actually do some flying.
Other activities offered	Hang gliding instruction

TANDEM SKYDIVING

Action Adventures Tandem Skydiving

Phone 0-9-232 6767 Freephone 0800 TO JUMP (0800 865 867) Mobile phone 025 941 756
Fax 0-9-233 6737 Email lyver@xtra.co.nz

Discounts	Group
Season	Year-round
Airfield	Mercer
Time to allow	1 hour
Bring with you	Comfortable outdoor clothing, sensible lace-up shoes
Cost	$195 (10,000 ft)
Optional extras	Video, action photo, T-shirt, hat, key ring
Operator's sales pitch	We have highly experienced tandem instructors.
Other activities offered	Tandem hang gliding

Parakai Parachute Centre

Phone 0-9-420 8064 Freephone 0800 753 000 Fax 0-9-420 8010 Email c.pine@xtra.co.nz

Discounts	NZ Outside, group
Season	Year-round
Airfield	Parakai
Time to allow	1.5 hours
Bring with you	Comfortable outdoor clothing, sensible shoes, small camera
Cost	$195 (10,000 ft)
Optional extras	Video, action photo
Operator's sales pitch	This is the only skydiving centre in New Zealand where you can see both the east and west coasts of the North Island from under the parachute. You'll also see the Hauraki Gulf islands and Auckland City.

THAMES

ABSEILING

Adventure Abseiling

Phone 0-7-868 7181 Mobile phone 025 726 627 Fax 0-7-868 7181 Email **abseil@amcom.co.nz**

Discounts	Group, Gold Rush experience
Operator's sales pitch	The instructor's experience mixed with the love of working with people make this a fun, neat adventure. Instructor's positions with Search and Rescue and St John's Ambulance make the operation particularly safety-conscious.

Abseiling	
Location	Thames coast
Activity	Full safety briefing followed by 2 abseil descents or rap jumps
Season	Year-round
Time to allow	2–4 hours
Bring with you	Sensible shoes, jacket, drink
Cost	$35 (includes 2 descents)

PAUANUI BEACH

FLYING FOX

Johansen Guiding Adventures Ltd 430 Settlement Road, Pauanui Beach

Phone 0-7-864 8731 Mobile phone 025 982 509 Fax 0-7-864 8731
Email **adventures@coromandel.net.nz** Website **www.coromandel.net.nz**

Discounts	Kiwi Experience, NZ Outside, Global Explorer Travel Card
Season	Year-round
Time to allow	15 minutes
Ride time	17 seconds
Ride length	230 m
Maximum height	20 m
Bring with you	Sensible shoes
Cost	$27.50 (includes Burma bridges, suspended tunnel)
Operator's sales pitch	Ours is one of the longest flying foxes in the country.
Other activities offered	Hiking, scenic tours, glowworm tours, 4WD safari, camping, hunting, ropes and challenge course, team building, surfing trips

NGARUAWAHIA

GUIDED ADVENTURES

The Hole Adventure Pipiwai Farm, Matira Road, Matira

Phone 0-7-825 4515 Mobile phone 025 270 9673 Fax 0-7-825 4561 Email srworsp@xtra.co.nz

Discounts	Group, family, ISAC
Operator's sales pitch	The Hole Adventure has a wide variety of activities, including accommodation. We offer personal attention in a non-commercial atmosphere. There is a minimum of 4 people for most activities.
Other activities offered	Dog trial (people are dogs), swamp crossing, claybird shooting

Stalactite cave abseil combo

Location	Pipiwai Farm
Activity	Abseil more than 20 m into the mouth of the beautiful stalactite cave. Travel 300 m into the cave to the "Elephant's Foot" and return.
Season	Year-round
Time to allow	2.5–3 hours
Bring with you	Sensible shoes with good grip, moderate clothing
Cost	$55

Glowworm cave abseil combo

Location	Pipiwai Farm
Activity	Choice of abseil: 15 m or 40 m. Enter the cave through the squeeze (crawl for 10 m). Work your way into the main caverns, which are full of glowworms.
Season	Year-round
Time to allow	2.5–3 hours
Bring with you	Sensible shoes with good grip, moderate clothing
Cost	$55

Jurassic stroll in harness

Location	Pipiwai Farm
Activity	Abseil into a steep bushclad gully, a cave that collapsed hundreds of thousands of years ago. View old stalactites covered in moss, pass through small cave, cross 2 rope bridges then fly the 220 m flying fox. Take a quick trip into the stalactite cave.
Season	Year-round
Time to allow	4–6 hours
Bring with you	Sensible shoes with good grip, moderate clothing
Cost	$95 (includes light refreshments)

MATAMATA

TANDEM SKYDIVING

Skydive Waikato

Phone 0-7-888 8763 Freephone 0800 JUMP 77 (0800 586 777) Mobile phone 025 940 207
Email eric@freefall.co.nz Website www.freefall.co.nz

Discounts	Student
Season	Year-round
Airfields	Matamata, Kaipara Flats, Pauanui
Time to allow	1.5 hours
Bring with you	Comfortable outdoor clothing, sensible shoes
Cost	$185 (10,000 ft)
Optional extras	Video, action photo, T-shirt, cap
Operator's sales pitch	Ours is a low-volume, high-quality drop zone with great views. We offer personal service. Tandem jumpers get a $50 credit towards a solo jump.
Other activities offered	Gliding, scenic flights, accommodation

CAMBRIDGE

JETBOATING

Camjet

Phone 0-7-849 1232 Freephone 0800 CAMJET (0800 226 538) Mobile phone 025 278 9182
Email jane.lawrence@xtra.co.nz

Discounts	YHA, group, family, student
Season	Year-round
Departures	On demand
Launch site	Riverside Park
Time to allow	45 minutes
Time on water	30–40 minutes
Bring with you	Jacket if cool, camera
Cost	$45
Optional extras	Action photo
Operator's sales pitch	Jet with us through scenic native bush, waterfalls and mild rapids. We give you a historical commentary and take you through exhilarating jetboat manoeuvres.
Other activities offered	Picnic or BBQ trips for groups

ADVENTURE CAVING

Black Water "Rafting"®

Phone 0-7-878 6219 Freephone 0800 CAVING (0800 228 464) Fax 0-7-878 5190
Email bwr@blackwaterrafting.co.nz Website www.blackwaterrafting.co.nz

Discounts	Kiwi Experience, Magic Bus, group, family
Season	Year-round
Optional extras	Clothing
Operator's sales pitch	Yes, we are the original – and still the most popular – cave tubing tour company. We offer the most in the way of downstream floating and glowworms. We have great facilities and add-ons: showers, soup/bagels and admission to the Waitomo Museum of Caves.
Other activities offered	Dry cave trip using an inflatable raft

Black Water "Rafting" 1

Time to allow	3 hours
Time in cave	1 hour
Caving elements	Tube rafting, swim, jump, glowworms, river float
Bring with you	Towel, swimsuit, soap, shampoo
Cost	$65 (includes shower, snack, museum admission)

Black Water "Rafting" 2

Time to allow	4–5 hours
Time in cave	2–2.5 hours
Caving elements	Squeeze, abseil, Tyrolean traverse, tube rafting, swim, jump, slide, climb, glowworms, waterfalls
Bring with you	Towel, swimsuit, soap, shampoo
Cost	$125 (includes food, shower, museum admission)

Long Tomo Rafting

Phone 0-7-873 8012 Freephone 0800 CAVERAFT (0800 228 372)

Season	Year-round
Operator's sales pitch	We offer a top-quality caving experience at a budget price. Our guides are trained to the Waitomo standard.

Long tomo rafting

Time to allow	5 hours
Time in cave	1.5–2.5 hours
Caving elements	Squeeze, abseil, inflatable tubes/rafts, swim, jump, climb, glowworms
Bring with you	Towel, swimsuit, camera, spare pair of socks
Cost	$65 (includes shower)

Waitomo Adventures

Phone 0-7-878 7788 Freephone 0800 WAITOMO (0800 924 866) Fax 0-7-878 6266
Email bookings@waitomo.co.nz Website www.waitomo.co.nz

Discounts	VIP, YHA, Kiwi Experience, Magic Bus, NZ Outside, group, student
Season	Year-round
Optional extras	Action photo, T-shirt, souvenirs
Operator's sales pitch	We are the only adventure caving company to have won its class at the New Zealand Tourism Awards. We offer the most adventurous activities and the best safety record of any adventure caving company.

Tumu tumu toobing

Time to allow	4 hours
Time in cave	2 hours
Caving elements	Ladder, tube rafting, swim, jump, climb, glowworms
Bring with you	Towel, swimsuit
Cost	$65 (includes chocolate bar, shower)

Haggas honking holes

Time to allow	4 hours
Time in cave	2 hours
Caving elements	3 abseils, ladder, climb, glowworms – the most concentrated action
Bring with you	Towel, swimsuit
Cost	$125 (includes chocolate bar, shower, poster)

Lost world

Time to allow	4 hours
Time in cave	2 hours
Caving elements	100-m abseil, 30-m ladder, climb, glowworms
Bring with you	Warm outdoor clothing
Cost	$195 (includes chocolate bar, poster)

Lost world 7-hour

Time to allow	8 hours
Time in cave	6–7 hours
Caving elements	Abseil, swim, jump, climb, glowworms – New Zealand's ultimate caving adventure
Bring with you	Towel, swimsuit
Cost	$295 (includes lunch underground, dinner, shower, poster)

SELF-DRIVE JETBOATING

Woodlyn Park 1177 Waitomo Valley Road, Waitomo Caves

Phone 0-7-878 6666 Mobile phone 025 277 2555 Fax 0-7-878 8866
Email woodlyn_park@xtra.co.nz

Season	Year-round
Departures	On demand
Launch site	Woodlyn Park
Time to allow	5 minutes
Time on water	Varies: 1.5 km of figure 8 course
Cost	$35
Operator's sales pitch	You get to drive a jetboat capable of over 100 hp around islands and under a bridge – it's a real adrenalin rush.
Other activities offered	Pioneer heritage stage show, Pink Gumboot Cave adventure

GUIDED ADVENTURES

Waimarino Adventure Park Taniwha Place, Bethlehem, Tauranga

Phone 0-7-576 4233 Fax 0-7-576 1203 Email **waimarino@xtra.co.nz** Website **www.kayaks.co.nz**

Discounts	YHA, Kiwi Experience, group, family, schools
Operator's sales pitch	Waimarino Park is an outdoor adventure theme park in a unique, tranquil, beautiful location. Try your hand at abseiling, rap jumping, rock climbing, canyoning, flying fox, whitewater kayaking, kayak slide, Tarzan & Jane swing, gladiators pole, slip & slide, cargo net, rope climbing, balance wire.

Waimarino adventure

Location	Waimarino Adventure Park
Activity	Use of all facilities
Season	Year-round
Time to allow	3–6 hours
Bring with you	Food, drink, towel, outdoor clothing
Cost	$30 (includes equipment, basic instruction, supervision)

Wild Water xtreme

Location	Kaituna or Wairoa River
Activity	Share a topolino duo kayak with a guide and take on grade 5 whitewater.
Season	Year-round
Time to allow	4 hours
Bring with you	Warm change of clothes, towel, swimsuit
Cost	$155 (includes transport, thermals, wetsuit if needed)

LUGE

Papamoa Adventure Park 1162 Welcome Bay Road, Papamoa

Phone 0-7-542 0972 Mobile phone 025 982 354 Fax 0-7-542 0972
Email **papamoa.adventure.park@xtra.co.nz**

Discounts	Group
Season	Year-round
Time to allow	30 minutes
Bring with you	Sensible shoes
Cost	$25 (includes 3 luge rides, park entrance, complimentary games, hot drinks)
Operator's sales pitch	It's a world first: dirt track luge. It is an extremely thrilling ride in specially made carts that can reach up to 90 kph. Because the track is clay the carts drift on the corners. The top offers spectacular views of the Bay of Plenty region.
Other activities offered	Horse trekking, paintball game, 4WD motorbikes, target shooting, grass skiing, Argo (all terrain vehicle)

TANDEM SKYDIVING

Tauranga Tandem Skydiving

Phone 0-7-576 7990 Mobile phone 025 968 408 Fax 0-7-576 7934 Email freefall@xtra.co.nz

Discounts	YHA, Kiwi Experience, Magic Bus
Season	Year-round
Airfield	Tauranga
Time to allow	1 hour
Bring with you	Comfortable outdoor clothing, sensible shoes
Cost	$190 (8000 ft)
Optional extras	Video, action photo, T-shirt
Operator's sales pitch	This is a smaller, more personal drop zone located by New Zealand's best beaches.
Other activities offered	Vintage aircraft flights, scenic flights

MT MAUNGANUI

SWIMMING WITH DOLPHINS

Dolphin Seafaris

Freephone 0800 ECOTRIP (0800 326 874) Mobile phone 025 960 633 Fax 0-7-575 7367

Season	Year-round
Chance of seeing dolphins	95%
Chance of swimming with dolphins	90%
Guarantee	None
Likely marine life seen	Common and bottlenose dolphins, occasionally Hector's dolphins, whales, orcas, blue penguins and other seabirds, fish
Maximum number of swimmers	Groups of 6 at a time
Time to allow	3–4 hours
Time in water	30–60 minutes
Bring with you	Towel, swimsuit, sunscreen, camera, jacket in winter
Cost	$85 (includes refreshments)
Optional extras	T-shirt
Operator's sales pitch	We generally try to operate on optimum days when the odds of finding dolphins and swimming with them is high. This is meant to be a fun experience. Rough weather is no fun for anyone and the dolphins are very hard to find with a sea running.
Other activities offered	Game fishing (marlin, tuna, kingfish)

TE PUKE
JETBOATING

Longridge Jet at Longridge Funpark SH 33, Paengaroa (midway between Tauranga and Rotorua)

Phone 0-7-533 1515 Freephone 0800 TOPFUN (0800 867 386) Fax 0-7-533 1814
Email topfun@longridgepark.co.nz Website www.jetboating.co.nz

Discounts	VIP, YHA, Kiwi Experience, Magic Bus, group, family
Season	Year-round
Departures	Hourly
Launch site	Longridge Fun Park
Time to allow	45 minutes
Time on water	30 minutes
Cost	$59
Optional extras	Action photo, T-shirt, postcards
Operator's sales pitch	We are the North Island's most scenic and thrilling jetboat experience. The natural beauty of the Kaituna River, combined with the adrenalin rush of high-speed jetboating, is not to be missed!
Other activities offered	Combos (rafting, hillhoppers 4WD, helicopter)

WHAKATANE
JETBOATING

Kiwi Jet Boat Tours

Phone 0-7-307 0663 Freephone 0800 800 538 Fax 0-7-307 0663 Email KIWIJET@xtra.co.nz

Discounts	Group
Season	Year-round
Departures	On demand
Launch site	Matahina Dam
Time to allow	1.25 hours
Time on water	1–1.25 hours
Cost	$60 (if 4 or more passengers)
Operator's sales pitch	Owner/operator Bill Roberts is 4 times New Zealand jetboat champion and a past world champion. This is a *real* jetboat tour.

SWIMMING WITH DOLPHINS

Dolphins Down Under

Phone 0-7-308 4636 Freephone 0800 FLIPPER (0800 354 773) Fax 0-7-308 0359
Email dolphinswim@dolphinswim.co.nz Website www.dolphinswim.co.nz

Discounts	Direct bookings
Season	Year-round
Chance of seeing dolphins	95%
Chance of swimming with dolphins	95%
Guarantee	None
Likely marine life seen	Common dolphins, orcas, whales, sharks, fish, seals, gannets and other seabirds
Maximum number of swimmers	20
Time to allow	3–4 hours
Time in water	Up to 60 minutes
Bring with you	Towel, swimsuit, warm jacket
Cost	$100 (includes shower)
Operator's sales pitch	It is estimated that we have 15,000–20,000 resident dolphins in the Bay of Plenty. Our water visibility often exceeds 30–50 m, and the sea temperature is comparatively warm year-round.
Other activities offered	Scuba diving at White Island

WHITEWATER RAFTING

Motu River Expeditions

Phone 0-7-308 7760 Mobile phone 025 570 256 Fax 0-7-308 7760 Email moturaft@wave.co.nz

Optional extras	Action photo, T-shirt
Season	Year-round
Operator's sales pitch	Motu River Expeditions is a small operation – we keep it that way to give you, the customer, our personal service.

Rangitaiki River

River grade	3–4
Meeting point	Murupara
Time to allow	5 hours
Time on water	1.5–2 hours
Bring with you	Towel, swimsuit, runners, light jacket or sweater
Cost	$85 (includes BBQ lunch)

Wairoa River (dam controlled)

River grade	5
Meeting point	Poripori Road, Kaimais
Time to allow	4 hours
Time on water	1.5 hours
Bring with you	Towel, swimsuit, runners, light jacket or sweater
Cost	$80

Motu River

River grade	4 plus
Meeting point	Whakatane
Time to allow	8 hours
Time on water	5 hours approx.
Bring with you	Towel, swimsuit, running shoes, light jacket, warm sweater (includes helicopter, lunch, jetboat, transport)

OPOTIKI

JETBOATING

Motu River Jet and Eastern Bay Jet Boat Tours

Phone 0-7-315 8107 Freephone 0800 MOTU JET (0800 668 853) Mobile phone 025 958 306
Fax 0-7-315 8107

Discounts	Group, family
Season	Year-round
Departures	Regular and on demand
Launch site	SH 1, under Motu Bridge
Time to allow	2.5 hours
Time on water	Varies: 20 minutes–2.5 hours
Bring with you	Good footwear, sunglasses, warm outdoor clothing
Cost	$85 (includes short bush walk)
Optional extras	T-shirt
Operator's sales pitch	Our river, the Motu, is designated as a wilderness zone, totally protected by a special act of parliament. It is the only river to have this honour.
Other activities offered	Hunting, kayaking, rafting

ROTORUA

BUNGY JUMPING

Rotorua Bungy Agrodome Adventure Park, Western Road, Ngongotaha

Phone 0-7-357 4747 Freephone 0800 2 BUNGY (0800 228 649) Mobile phone 025 293 5544
Fax 0-7-357 4259 Email bungy@ihug.co.nz Website www.agrodome.co.nz

Discounts	Kiwi Experience, Magic Bus, group
Season	Year-round
Time to allow	10 minutes
Bungy height	43 m
Water entry available	No
Cost	$90 (includes T-shirt, certificate)
Optional extras	Video, action photo, T-shirt, hat
Operator's sales pitch	There's no walking or climbing involved. Jump above Ngongotaha River with views of Lake Rotorua. Tandem jumps are available.
Other activities offered	Giant swing, jet-sprint, helicopter, dirtboards, Zorb, Agrodome

FLYING FOX

Skyline Skyrides Gondola, Restaurant and Luge Fairy Springs Road, Rotorua

Phone 0-7-347 0027 Fax 0-7-348 2163
Email enquiries@skylineskyrides.co.nz Website www.skylineskyrides.co.nz

Discounts	Group, family
Season	Year-round
Time to allow	5–10 minutes
Ride time	3–4 minutes
Ride length	500 m
Maximum height	8 m
Bring with you	Sensible shoes
Cost	$4.50
Operator's sales pitch	Our flying fox zigzags across the luge track and you return to the top via the chairlift.
Other activities offered	Sidewinder, luge, walking track, food outlets

GIANT SWING

Swoop Agrodome Adventure Park, Western Road, Ngongotaha

Phone 0-7-357 4747 Freephone 0800 2 BUNGY (0800 228 649) Mobile phone 025 293 5544
Fax 0-7-357 4259 Email bungy@ihug.co.nz Website www.agrodome.co.nz

Discounts	Kiwi Experience, Magic Bus, group
Season	Year-round
Time to allow	10 minutes
Bungy height	40 m
Cost	$30–$45 depending on numbers
Optional extras	Action photo, T-shirt, hat
Operator's sales pitch	1, 2 or 3 people are placed in hang gliding harnesses, raised to a height of 40 m. Pull the rip-cord and experience the feeling of flying, reaching speeds of 130 kph and a G-force factor of 3.
Other activities offered	Bungy, jet-sprint, helicopter, dirtboards, Zorb, Agrodome

JET-SPRINTING

Agrojet Agrodome Adventure Park, Western Road, Ngongotaha

Phone 0-7-357 2929 Freephone 0800 AGROJET (0800 247 653) Mobile phone 025 727 032
Fax 0-7-357 4259 Email agrojet@xtra.co.nz Website www.agrodome.co.nz

Discounts	Kiwi Experience, Magic Bus, group, family
Season	Year-round
Departures	On demand
Launch site	Agrodome Adventure Park
Time to allow	5 minutes
Time on water	5 minutes
Cost	$25–$35
Optional extras	Action photo, hat
Operator's sales pitch	Our jet-sprint boats are much faster and more manoeuvrable than standard jetboats, with 450 hp in a 13-ft boat as opposed to 300 hp in an 18-ft standard jet. Get ready for major thrills.
Other activities offered	Bungy, giant swing, helicopter, dirtboards, Zorb, Agrodome

LUGE

Skyline Skyrides Gondola, Restaurant and Luge Fairy Springs Road, Rotorua

Phone 0-7-347 0027 Fax 0-7-348 2163
Email enquiries@skylineskyrides.co.nz Website www.skylineskyrides.co.nz

Discounts	Group, family
Season	Year-round
Time to allow	1 hour
Cost	$22 (includes 5 luge rides, gondola)
Optional extras	T-shirt
Operator's sales pitch	A world first, the luge cart is specially designed. There is a choice of 2 tracks, scenic and advanced, situated on the side of Mt Ngongotaha. This is an all-age, all-weather attraction.
Other activities offered	Flying fox, sidewinder, food outlets, walking track

TANDEM SKYDIVING

Tandem Skydiving Rotorua

Phone 0-7-345 7520 Fax 0-7-345 7850 Email nzpf@xtra.co.nz

Discounts	VIP, YHA, Kiwi Experience, Magic Bus, group
Season	Year-round
Airfield	Rotorua
Time to allow	1 hour
Bring with you	Comfortable outdoor clothing, sensible shoes
Cost	$180 (9500 ft)
Optional extras	Video, action photo, T-shirt
Operator's sales pitch	We offer personal service, a professional approach and an excellent safety record.
Other activities offered	Accelerated freefall over 2 days ($295), aerobatic flights

WHITEWATER KAYAKING

Kaituna Cascades

Phone 0-7-357 5032 Freephone 0800 KAITUNA (0800 524 886) Fax 0-7-357 4370
Email kaituna.cascades@clear.net.nz

Discounts	Kiwi Experience, NZ Outside, group, family
Optional extras	Video, action photo, T-shirt
Season	Year-round
Operator's sales pitch	We were the first in the country to offer tandem kayaks. You take the front seat, the guides take the back, and together you take on the falls and drops of the Kaituna River.
Other activities offered	Whitewater rafting

Kaituna River (tandem)

River grade	5
Put-in point	Okere Falls
Time to allow	2.5 hours
Time on water	50 minutes
Bring with you	Towel, swimsuit
Cost	$95

Kaituna Cascades *(continued)*	
Rangitaiki River (Aniwhenua Falls)	
River grade	2 with waterfall
Put-in point	Aniwhenua Falls
Time to allow	6 hours
Time on water	3 hours
Bring with you	Towel, swimsuit
Cost	$125 (intro course)

WHITEWATER RAFTING

Great Kiwi Whitewater Co.

Phone 0-7-348 2144 Mobile phone 025 872 910 Fax 0-7-348 1238

Discounts	VIP, YHA, Kiwi Experience, Magic Bus, NZ Outside, group, family
Optional extras	Action photo, T-shirt, hat, towels
Season	Year-round
Operator's sales pitch	We cater from mild to wild trips, with safety and enjoyment our aim.

Rangitaiki River	
River grade	2–4
Put-in point	Murupara
Time to allow	5.5–6 hours
Time on water	1.5–2 hours
Bring with you	Towel, swimsuit
Cost	$89 (includes transport ex Rotorua, lunch, shower)

Kaituna River	
River grade	3–5
Put-in point	Okere Falls
Time to allow	2.5 hours
Time on water	40–50 minutes
Bring with you	Towel, swimsuit
Cost	$65 (includes transport ex Rotorua, shower)

Wairoa River (dam controlled)	
River grade	4–5
Put-in point	Near Tauranga
Time to allow	4–6 hours
Time on water	1.5–2 hours
Bring with you	Towel, swimsuit
Cost	$79 (includes transport ex Rotorua, lunch)

Kaituna Cascades

Phone 0-7-357 5032 Freephone 0800 KAITUNA (0800 524 886) Fax 0-7-357 4370
Email kaituna.cascades@clear.net.nz

Discounts	Kiwi Experience, NZ Outside, group, family
Optional extras	Video, action photo, T-shirt
Season	Year-round
Operator's sales pitch	We were the first to raft the Kaituna. Our rafts are custom-built and we will give you the safest, most enjoyable and best-equipped river trips on offer.
Other activities offered	Whitewater kayaking

Kaituna Cascades *(continued)*

Kaituna River

River grade	5
Put-in point	Okere Falls
Time to allow	2.5 hours
Time on water	50 minutes
Bring with you	Towel, swimsuit/shorts
Cost	$65

Wairoa River

River grade	5
Put-in point	McLaren Falls
Time to allow	3 hours
Time on water	1.75 hours
Bring with you	Towel, swimsuit
Cost	$72

Rangitaiki River

River grade	4
Put-in point	Kaingaroa Forest
Time to allow	5 hours
Time on water	2.25 hours
Bring with you	Towel, swimsuit
Cost	$85

Raftabout Wilderness Expeditions

Freephone **0800 RAFTABOUT (0800 723 822)**
Email **raftabout@xtra.co.nz** Website **www.raftabout.co.nz**

Discounts	Group
Optional extras	Action photo, T-shirt
Season	Year-round
Operator's sales pitch	Raftabout was born out of a need for a professional company with the highest possible standards in equipment and personnel.

Kaituna River

River grade	5
Put-in point	Okere Falls
Time to allow	2 hours
Time on water	45 minutes
Bring with you	Towel, swimsuit
Cost	$60 (includes transport)

Rangitaiki River

River grade	3–4
Put-in point	Kaingaroa Forest
Time to allow	5 hours
Time on water	1.5 hours
Bring with you	Towel, swimsuit
Cost	$89 (includes transport, lunch)

Raftabout Wilderness Expeditions *(continued)*

Wairoa River (dam controlled)

River grade	5
Put-in point	McLaren Falls
Time to allow	5 hours
Time on water	1.5 hours
Bring with you	Towel, swimsuit
Cost	$79 (includes lunch)

River Rats

Phone 0-7-345 6543 Freephone 0800 333 900 Fax 0-7-345 6321
Email info@riverrats.co.nz Website www.riverrats.co.nz

Discounts	Group, backpackers if booked through hostel
Optional extras	Video, action photo, T-shirt, cap
Season	Year-round
Operator's sales pitch	Our service is thoroughly professional and friendly, and our guides are motivated and enthusiastic. All equipment meets or exceeds New Zealand safety requirements. We spend longer on the water than other rafting companies and give you safe thrills and extreme fun.

Rangitaiki River

River grade	4
Put-in point	Murupara
Time to allow	6–6.5 hours
Time on water	1.5–2 hours
Bring with you	Towel, swimsuit
Cost	$89 (includes transport ex Rotorua, lunch)

Kaituna River

River grade	5
Put-in point	Okere Falls
Time to allow	2–2.5 hours
Time on water	45–55 minutes
Bring with you	Towel, swimsuit
Cost	$69 (includes transport ex Rotorua, 2 guides per raft)

Wairoa River (dam controlled)

River grade	5
Put-in point	McLaren Falls
Time to allow	3 hours
Time on water	1.5–1.75 hours
Bring with you	Towel, swimsuit
Cost	$79 (includes lunch)

Wet'nWild Rafting

Phone 0-7-348 3191 Freephone 0800 IN A RAFT (0800 462 723) Mobile phone 025 778 011
Fax 0-7-349 6567 Email wetnwild@wave.co.nz Website www.wave.co.nz/pages/wetnwild

Discounts	NZ Outside, group
Optional extras	T-shirt
Season	Year-round
Operator's sales pitch	Wet'n Wild rafting also specialises in a range of overnight expeditions on the Motu and Mohaka Rivers, ranging from 2 to 5 days.

Rangitaiki River

River grade	3–4
Put-in point	Murupara
Time to allow	6 hours
Time on water	2 hours
Bring with you	Personal clothing, towel, shoes optional
Cost	$85 (includes light refreshments, shower)

Kaituna River

River grade	5
Put-in point	Okere Falls
Time to allow	2.5 hours
Time on water	45 minutes
Bring with you	Personal clothing, towel, shoes optional
Cost	$65 (includes transport ex Rotorua, shower)

Wairoa River (dam controlled)

River grade	5
Put-in point	McLaren Falls
Time to allow	3 hours
Time on water	1.5 hours
Bring with you	Personal clothing, towel, shoes optional
Cost	$75

WHITEWATER SLEDGING

Kaitiaki Adventures

Phone 0-6-278 5555 Freephone 0800 338 736 Mobile phone 025 249 9481 Fax 0-6-278 5555
Website www.kaitiaki.co.nz

Discounts	VIP, YHA, group, family
Optional extras	T-shirt
Season	Year-round
Operator's sales pitch	Let us take you on a water sports experience you will never forget: action, adventure, adrenalin, culture and great rivers, great whitewater, great guides.

Rangitaiki River (Geoff's Joy)

River grade	2–4
Put-in point	Murupara
Time to allow	4–5 hours
Time on water	2–3 hours
Bring with you	Towel, swimsuit
Cost	$98 (includes transport ex Rotorua, refreshments, shower)

Kaitiaki Adventures *(continued)*

Kaituna River

River grade	5
Put-in point	Okere Falls
Time to allow	2.5–3 hours
Time on water	2.5 hours
Bring with you	Towel, swimsuit
Cost	$110 (includes transport ex Rotorua, refreshments, shower)

Wairoa River

River grade	5
Put-in point	McLaren Falls
Time to allow	4–5 hours
Time on water	4 hours
Bring with you	Towel, swimsuit
Cost	$110 (includes transport ex Rotorua, refreshments, shower)

ZORB

Zorb Rotorua Agrodome Adventure Park, Western Road, Ngongotaha

Phone **0-7-357 5100** Mobile phone **025 850 628** Fax **0-7-357 4259**
Email **rotorua@zorb.com** Website **www.zorb.com**

Discounts	Group
Season	Year-round
Time to allow	10 minutes
Cost	$40 (includes 1 ride; dry plus wet zorb for $60)
Optional extras	Video, action photo, T-shirt
Operator's sales pitch	Rotorua is the home of this Kiwi invention. Get harnessed inside for the Dry Zorb or go loose in the Wet Zorb on a 170-m revolutionary ride!
Other activities offered	Bungy, giant swing, jet-sprint, helicopter, dirtboards, Agrodome

TAUPO

BUNGY JUMPING

Taupo Bungy 202 Spa Road, Taupo

Freephone **0800 888 408** Email **jump@taupobungy.co.nz** Website **www.taupobungy.co.nz**

Discounts	NZ Outside, group
Season	Year-round
Time to allow	30 minutes–1 hour
Bungy height	47 m
Water entry available	Yes
Bring with you	Footwear for walk back
Cost	$89 (includes certificate)
Optional extras	Video, action photo, T-shirt
Operator's sales pitch	Take the plunge with Taupo Bungy. Located in the Waikato River valley upstream of Huka Falls, our cantilever platform sits 47m above the river. Jump solo or tandem. Want to chill out? Go for the water touch – the ultimate ground rush.
Other activities offered	Max Buzz combos (bungy, ropes course, tandem skydive)

HOT AIR BALLOONING

Balloons Are Fun

Phone 0-7-377 0660 Freephone 0800 FLY HAPPY (0800 359 427) Mobile phone 025 787 919
Fax 0-7-378 4671 Email info@biplane.co.nz

Discounts	VIP, YHA, Kiwi Experience, Magic Bus, group, family
Season	Year-round
Time to allow	4 hours
Flight time	1–1.5 hours
Bring with you	Warm outdoor clothing
Cost	$225 (includes transport, champagne breakfast)
Optional extras	Video, action photo, T-shirt
Operator's sales pitch	We consider our operation a boutique balloon company, catering more to individual requirements and specialising in "over water" balloon experiences.
Other activities offered	Geothermal Explorer, long-distance flights

JETBOATING

Huka Jet

Phone 0-7-374 8572 Freephone 0800 485 2538 Fax 0-7-374 8573
Email hukajet@xtra.co.nz Website www.hukajet.co.nz

Discounts	YHA, Magic Bus, NZ Outside, group, family
Season	Year-round
Departures	On demand
Launch site	Wairakei Tourist Park
Time to allow	1 hour
Time on water	30 minutes
Bring with you	Cameras but no videos, warm outdoor clothing, sunglasses
Cost	$55
Optional extras	Action photo, clothing
Operator's sales pitch	Enjoy half an hour of awesome jetboating along the beautiful Waikato River, with an amazing water-level view of the spectacular Huka Falls. There'll be fun and exhilaration and lots of 360° spins.
Other activities offered	Heli-jet (10–12 minutes helicopter plus 30 minutes jetboat)

Rapids Jet

Phone 0-7-378 5828 Freephone 0800 RAPIDS (0800 727 437) Fax 0-7-378 3828
Email rapids@xtra.co.nz

Discounts	VIP, YHA, Kiwi Experience, Magic Bus, NZ Outside, group, family
Season	Year-round
Departures	Hourly
Launch site	Rapids Road, Aratiatia
Time to allow	45 minutes
Time on water	40 minutes
Cost	$55
Optional extras	Action photo, T-shirt, hat
Operator's sales pitch	We jetboat New Zealand's biggest commercially jetboated rapids both upstream and down.
Other activities offered	Combo with *New Zealand African Queen*

ROPES COURSE

Rock'n Ropes Crazy Catz Adventure Park, SH 5, Wairakei

Phone 0-7-374 8111 Freephone 0800 244 508 Mobile phone 025 274 8504 Fax 0-7-378 1351

Discounts	Group
Season	Year-round
Time to allow	4 hours
Bring with you	Sensible shoes, outdoor clothing
Cost	$59
Operator's sales pitch	Try a selection of truly unbelievable and brilliant high ropes activities, in an experience where groups become a team, strangers become friends and individuals come face to face with themselves.
Other activities offered	Giant swing on its own ($15), combo of giant swing, giant trapeze and high beam ($35), Max Buzz combos (bungy, ropes course, tandem skydive)

TANDEM SKYDIVING

Great Lake Skydive Centre

Phone 0-7-378 4662 Freephone 0800 FREEFLY (0800 373 335) Fax 0-7-377 4851
Email greg@freefly.co.nz Website www.freefly.co.nz

Discounts	Kiwi Experience, group
Season	Year-round
Airfield	Taupo
Time to allow	1.5 hours
Bring with you	Comfortable outdoor clothing, sensible shoes
Cost	$165 (9000 ft)
Optional extras	Video, action photos, merchandise
Operator's sales pitch	This is New Zealand's family drop zone, the most scenic in the world. You can make the highest tandem skydive available – oxygen-assisted from 15,000 ft. We offer first-class service, safety and professionalism and we can take disabled people.
Other activities offered	Accelerated freefall over 1 day. All skydiving related business.

Taupo Tandem Skydiving

Phone 0-7-377 0428 Freephone 0800 2 SKYDIVE (0800 275 934) bookings Fax 0-7-378 0468
Email skydive@skydive.net.nz Website www.skydive.net.nz

Season	Year-round
Airfield	Taupo
Time to allow	2 hours
Bring with you	Comfortable outdoor clothing, sensible shoes
Cost	$165 (9000 ft)
Optional extras	Digital video, digital action photos, full range of merchandise
Operator's sales pitch	We have a large, comfortable twin-engine plane, so we can take up to 7 tandems in one group. We have very competitive rates, and there is an alcohol/drug testing programme for staff.
Other activities offered	Accelerated freefall over 1 day ($325), Max Buzz combos (bungy, ropes course, tandem skydive)

WHITEWATER RAFTING

Kiwi River Safaris

Phone 0-7-377 6597 Freephone 0800 RAFT KRS (0800 723 857) Mobile phone 025 220 4608
Fax 0-7-377 6572 Email rafting@krs.co.nz Website www.krs.co.nz

Discounts	Group, family
Optional extras	Video, action photo, T-shirt
Season	Year-round
Operator's sales pitch	KRS guides are dedicated to showing you an excellent day on the river. We take the time to surf in the holes, swim in the calm spots and play in all the favourite spots.

Rangitaiki River

River grade	3–4
Put-in point	Murupara
Time to allow	3.5–4 hours ex Murupara, 5.5 hours ex Taupo
Time on water	2 hours
Bring with you	Towel, swimsuit, sunscreen
Cost	$85 (includes transport ex Taupo, lunch)

Wairoa River (dam controlled)

River grade	4–5
Put-in point	McLaren Falls
Time to allow	3 hours
Time on water	2 hours
Bring with you	Towel, swimsuit, sunscreen
Cost	$85 (includes transport ex Taupo, lunch)

TURANGI

WHITEWATER KAYAKING

Eddyline Adventures

Phone 0-7-386 5081 Freephone 0800 UKAYAK (0800 852 925) Fax 0-7-386 5081
Email edline@reap.org.nz

Discounts	NZ Outside
Season	October–April
Operator's sales pitch	Our kayaking trips use inflatable kayaks, which are more stable, safer and easier to paddle than ordinary kayaks. All trips are guided.
Other activities offered	Trips on grade 3 whitewater for kayakers with experience.

Tongariro River (inflatable kayaks)

River grade	2
Put-in point	Breakaway Pool
Time to allow	3 hours
Time on water	1.5 hours
Bring with you	Towel, swimsuit
Cost	$58 (includes transport)

WHITEWATER RAFTING

Rapid Sensations

Phone 0-7-378 7902 Freephone 0800 22 RAFT (0800 227 238) Fax 0-7-378 7904
Email info@rapids.co.nz Website www.rapids.co.nz

Discounts	Group
Optional extras	Action photo (sometimes), T-shirt
Season	Year-round
Operator's sales pitch	We have a reputation as a small, highly professional rafting operator with a commitment to providing the highest quality experience possible.
Other activities offered	Rafting/fly fishing trips

Tongariro River

River grade	3
Put-in point	Poutu intake
Time to allow	4 hours ex Turangi, 6 hours ex Taupo
Time on water	2.25 hours
Bring with you	Towel, swimsuit, sunscreen
Cost	$80 (includes transport ex Taupo and Turangi, lunch, shower)

Rangitaiki River (Geoff's Joy)

River grade	3–4
Put-in point	Above Geoff's Joy
Time to allow	6 hours ex Taupo
Time on water	1.2–2 hours
Bring with you	Towel, swimsuit, sunscreen
Cost	$85 (includes transport ex Taupo and Turangi, lunch, shower)

Wairoa River (dam controlled)

River grade	4–5
Put-in point	McLaren Falls
Time to allow	3–4 hours
Time on water	1.5 hours
Bring with you	Towel, swimsuit, sunscreen
Cost	$75 (includes transport ex Taupo and Turangi, lunch, shower)

Mangahao River

River grade	4
Put-in point	No. 2 dam
Time to allow	Full day
Time on water	4–5 hours
Bring with you	Towel, swimsuit, sunscreen
Cost	$195 (includes helicopter, lunch, shower)

River Rats

Phone 0-7-345 6543 Freephone 0800 333 900 Fax 0-7-345 6321
Email info@riverrats.co.nz Website www.riverrats.co.nz

Discounts	Group (by arrangement)
Optional extras	Action photo, T-shirt, cap
Season	Year-round
Operator's sales pitch	Our service is thoroughly professional and friendly, and our guides are motivated and enthusiastic. Equipment meets or exceeds New Zealand safety requirements.
Other activities offered	Scenic family whitewater rafting, combos with local attractions

Tongariro River

River grade	3
Put-in point	Turangi
Time to allow	3–3.5 hours
Time on water	2–2.5 hours
Bring with you	Towel, swimsuit
Cost	$75 (includes transport ex Turangi, lunch, entry to hot pools in winter)

NATIONAL PARK ▶

GUIDED ADVENTURES

Pete Outdoors

Phone 0-7-892 2773 Fax 0-7-892 2775 Email PeteOutdoors@xtra.co.nz

Discounts	NZ Outside
Operator's sales pitch	We are a small family-owned and operated business. We prefer to work with small groups and offer a good quality product with top service and a high safety standard. Activities require a minimum of 2 people.
Other activities offered	Guided tramps, mountain bike hire and guided rides

Abseiling/rock climbing

Location	Tongariro National Park
Activity	Get an introduction to and coaching in abseiling and rock climbing. Learn about equipment and techniques, then practise them.
Season	Year-round
Time to allow	Half day
Bring with you	Tramping or sports shoes
Cost	$50 (includes transport; gourmet lunch available – $20 extra)

Caving

Location	Tongariro forest
Activity	Go underground and explore: follow a stream, climb into caverns, experience some squeezes, see glowworms and cave wetas. This is a great introduction to "hands-on" caving. We guarantee you will get wet and dirty.
Season	Year-round
Time to allow	Half day
Bring with you	Food, footwear
Cost	$60 (includes transport; gourmet lunch available – $20 extra)

GUIDED ADVENTURES

MacAlpine Guides

Phone 0-6-751 3542 Mobile phone 025 417 042 Fax 0-6-751 5026 Email guidemac@hotmail.com

Discounts	NZ Outside, group, family
Operator's sales pitch	Taranaki's leading mountain guiding and outdoor pursuits specialists. Offers clients a large range of outdoor activities to give a fun, safe, exciting trip into the New Zealand outdoors.
Other activities offered	Mountaineering, kayaking, hiking, confidence course, flying fox, team building

Abseiling

Location	White Cliffs, Urenui
Activity	Abseiling down 50-m sea cliffs – a beautiful photo opportunity. This is a worthwhile event.
Season	Year-round
Time to allow	1 hour
Bring with you	Sensible shoes, jacket, camera
Cost	$30

Bridge swinging

Location	Bertrand Road bridge
Activity	Bridge swinging is an adventure activity, a sort of gentle bungy. The rope is tied on one side of the bridge, goes under the bridge and up the other side and is clipped onto a harness. Then you let go of the bridge and pendulum.
Season	Year-round
Time to allow	1 hour
Bring with you	Warm clothes, maybe wetsuit
Cost	$30

Rock climbing

Location	Paritutu Rock
Activity	Paritutu, New Plymouth, has rock climbing that is ideal for beginners.
Season	December–April
Time to allow	Half day
Bring with you	Warm clothes, jacket, food and drink
Cost	By arrangement

Mountaineering

Location	Mt Taranaki
Activity	Climb to the summit of this dramatic volcano.
Season	Year-round
Time to allow	Full day
Bring with you	Warm clothing, hiking boots
Cost	By arrangement

Wildest Dreams

Freephone/Fax **0800 151 589** Mobile phone **025 248 7858**
Email **wildest.dreams@xtra.co.nz**

Discounts	NZ Outside
Operator's sales pitch	Run by accredited guide Don Paterson, Wildest Dreams is a small company that has the versatility and flexibility to adapt or change a programme to meet most people's needs.
Other activities offered	Alpine instruction and guiding, bush walks, ropes/confidence course, whitewater rafting, whitewater kayaking

Abseiling/rap jumping

Location	Sites around New Plymouth
Activity	Abseil over cliffs, waterfalls or buildings.
Season	Year-round
Time to allow	1–4 hours
Bring with you	By arrangement
Cost	By arrangement

Rock climbing

Location	Paritutu or Mt Taranaki
Activity	Learn how to rock climb.
Season	Year-round
Time to allow	2–10 hours
Bring with you	By arrangement
Cost	By arrangement

Bridge swinging

Location	Waitara River
Activity	Get an adrenalin rush as you jump off a bridge and start to pendulum, just avoiding the river.
Season	Year-round
Time to allow	1 hour
Cost	$25 (includes 2 jumps)

HAWERA

WHITEWATER SLEDGING

Kaitiaki Adventures

Phone 0-6-278 5555 Freephone 0800 DAM DROP (0800 326 376) Mobile phone 021 461 110
Fax 0-6-278 5555 Email darrenparata@hotmail.com Website www.kaitiaki.co.nz

Discounts	VIP, YHA, group, family
Optional extras	T-shirt
Season	Year-round
Operator's sales pitch	Let us take you on a water sports experience you will never forget: action, adventure, adrenalin, culture and great rivers, great whitewater, great guides.

Waingongoro River

River grade	1–3
Put-in point	Powerco Aquatic Centre, Hawera
Time to allow	3 hours
Time on water	2.25 hours
Bring with you	Towel, swimsuit
Cost	$80 (includes transport from pool, refreshments, shower)

WAITOTARA

JETBOATING

Remote Adventures

Phone 0-6-346 5747 Fax 0-6-346 6033 Website www.remoteadventures.co.nz

Discounts	Group, family
Season	Year-round
Departures	On demand
Time to allow	1–2.5 hours
Time on water	50 minutes
Cost	$58 (includes refreshments)
Operator's sales pitch	Jetboat into the rugged, uninhabited upper reaches of the Waitotara River through sub-tropical rainforest. View pioneer work and take a short walk to a beautiful waterfall.
Other activities offered	Farm stays, scenic flights, 4WD tours, farm tours

TAIHAPE

WHITEWATER RAFTING

River Valley Ventures

Phone 0-6-388 1444 Fax 0-6-388 1859
Email thelodge@rivervalley.co.nz Website www.rivervalley.co.nz

Discounts	Kiwi Experience, NZ Outside
Season	Year-round
Activity	Whitewater rafting
Optional extras	Action photo, T-shirt
Operator's sales pitch	Riverside Lodge, where people meet and the trip ends, has accommodation, meals and a bar all on site. Ours is the top whitewater trip in the North Island.
Other activities offered	Abseiling, accommodation

Rangitikei River

River grade	5
Put-in point	Pukeokahu
Time to allow	4–5 hours
Time on water	2.5–3 hours
Bring with you	Towel, swimsuit
Cost	$95 (includes shuttle from lodge, chocolate bar)

MANGAWEKA

BUNGY JUMPING

High Time Bungy Torere Road, Mokai Bridge, Mangaweka

Freephone 0800 80 BUNGY (0800 802 864) Fax 0-6-388 1618 Email ht-bungy@ihug.co.nz

Season	Year-round
Time to allow	10–15 minutes
Bungy height	80 m
Water entry available	No
Cost	$99
Optional extras	Video, action photo, T-shirt
Operator's sales pitch	We are jumping into a very narrow gorge over the Rangitikei River. You are lifted back up to the bridge by the only water-powered, counter-balanced chairlift in the world.

JET-SPRINTING

Flat Hills Sprint Jet Flat Hills Park, Mangaweka

Phone 0-6-322 9734 Fax 0-6-322 9712

Discounts	Magic Bus, group, family
Season	Year-round
Departures	On demand
Launch site	Flat Hills Park
Time to allow	5 minutes
Time on water	5 minutes
Cost	$25
Operator's sales pitch	Ours is New Zealand's first purpose-built commercial jet-sprinting complex. We'll take you jet-sprinting in a genuine, high-powered race boat.
Other activities offered	Offroad buggies

GISBORNE

SWIMMING WITH SHARKS

Surfit Shark Cage Experience

Phone 0-6-867 2970 Mobile phone 025 307 216 Fax 0-6-867 2703
Email surfit.enterprises@xtra.co.nz

Discounts	Group, family
Season	November–April
Chance of swimming with sharks	95%
Guarantee	50% refund if no sharks seen
Likely marine life seen	Blue and mako sharks, dolphins, penguins, fish
Maximum number of swimmers	6
Time to allow	3–5 hours
Time in water	30 minutes
Bring with you	Towel, swimsuit
Cost	$150 (includes shower)
Optional extras	Video, action photo, T-shirt
Operator's sales pitch	Participants stand chest-deep in the shark cage, which is attached to the boat, grab a regulator and duck underwater to view the sharks.
Other activities offered	Fishing charters

NAPIER

WHITEWATER KAYAKING

Salty Rock Adventure Centre

Phone 0-6-834 3500 Fax 0-6-834 3502 Email saltyrock@clear.net.nz

Discounts	Kiwi Experience, Magic Bus, group, NZAC
Operator's sales pitch	Salty Rock has based itself in the heart of Hawke's Bay and is going where no man or woman has adventured before. We are a fresh team with brand-new toys to share!
Other activities offered	Canyoning, abseiling, caving, indoor rock climbing

Mohaka kayak adventure

Location	Mohaka River
Activity	Spend half a day paddling sit-on-top kayaks through grade 2 whitewater
Season	Year-round
Time to allow	6 hours
Bring with you	Thermals
Cost	$85 (includes transport, snacks, drink)

WHITEWATER RAFTING

Riverlands Outback Adventures

Phone 0-6-834 9756 Mobile phone 025 755 258 Fax 0-6-834 9724 Email riverlnds@xtra.co.nz

Discounts	Group, family
Optional extras	Video, action photo
Season	Year-round
Operator's sales pitch	We are the great outdoors: stunning scenery, exciting adventures, lodge accommodation. There's plenty of room for everyone to find tranquillity on 260 acres.
Other activities offered	Scenic family whitewater rafting, horse treks, kayaking, trout fishing, claybird shooting, abseiling/rock climbing, archery, orienteering, camping ground/accommodation

Mohaka River

River grade	3–4
Put-in point	Glenfalls Forest
Time to allow	7 hours
Time on water	5 hours
Bring with you	Towel, swimsuit
Cost	$80 (includes transport, lunch)

HAVELOCK NORTH

TANDEM PARAGLIDING

Peak Paragliding

Phone 0-6-877 8804 Mobile phone 025 223 6999
Email shaun.g@xtra.co.nz Website members.xoom.com/shaung

Season	Labour Weekend–Easter
Launch site	Te Mata Peak
Time to allow	30 minutes
Flight time	5–15 minutes
Bring with you	Comfortable outdoor clothing including windproof top, sensible shoes
Cost	$120 (includes certificate)
Operator's sales pitch	My flights are soaring flights with most landing back on the ridge. If conditions are ideal we can climb to the cloudbase.
Other activities offered	Cross-country flights, but these require special conditions – see website for details

WAIPUKURAU

HOT AIR BALLOONING

Early Morning Balloons Ltd

Phone 0-6-858 8480 Mobile phone 025 445 645 Fax 0-6-858 8480
Email quintinespie@xtra.co.nz Website www.early-am-balloons.co.nz

Discounts	Kiwi Experience, Magic Bus, group
Season	Year-round
Time to allow	4 hours
Flight time	1 hour
Bring with you	Warm outdoor clothing, camera, hat, sunglasses
Cost	$225 (includes transport, champagne breakfast)
Optional extras	Champagne glasses, cap
Operator's sales pitch	Hawke's Bay is the perfect region for ballooning, with wide, open spaces of farmlands, orchards, vineyards and a picturesque mountain background.

MASTERTON

JETBOATING

Wairarapa Jet Adventures

Phone 0-6-377 2114 Mobile phone 025 464 664 Fax 0-6-377 2114
Email waijet@wise.net.nz Website wairarapa.co.nz/jet-adventures

Season	Year-round
Departures	On demand
Launch sites	Ruamahanga River, Manawatu Gorge
Time to allow	2 hours
Time on water	30 minutes
Bring with you	Change of clothes
Cost	$35 (Ruamahanga), $45 (Manawatu) – requires 5 passengers
Operator's sales pitch	We operate smaller boats than large commercial operators and our skilled drivers give a very personalised trip. The Manawatu Gorge trip would have to be the best in New Zealand. Contact us for a quote if there are less than 5 in your group.

TANDEM SKYDIVING

Wairarapa Pilot and Parachute Centre

Phone 0-6-378 7309 Freephone 0800 TO SKYDIVE (0800 867 593) Mobile phone 025 428 805
Fax 0-6-370 8143 Email wpc@contact.net.nz Website www.wpc.co.nz

Discounts	Group, student
Season	Year-round
Airfield	Masterton
Time to allow	1 hour
Bring with you	Comfortable outdoor clothing, sensible shoes
Cost	$220 (9000 ft)
Optional extras	Action photo, T-shirt
Operator's sales pitch	We are the only skydiving outfit in the area operating full-time. We have full facilities, including bar, pool table and swimming pool.
Other activities offered	Accelerated freefall, flight training

CARTERTON

HOT AIR BALLOONING

Balloning New Zealand

Phone 0-6-379 8223 Mobile phone 025 224 8696 Fax 0-6-379 8223

Discounts	VIP, group
Season	Year-round
Time to allow	2–3 hours
Flight time	1 hour
Bring with you	Warm outdoor clothing, hat, sunglasses, warm socks, waterproof footwear in winter
Cost	$230 (includes champagne breakfast)
Optional extras	T-shirt
Operator's sales pitch	Enjoy the majesty of snow-capped mountains and the serenity of the scenic countryside from the peace and stillness of a hot-air balloon.

PAEKAKARIKI

FLY BY WIRE

Fly by Wire

Mobile phone 025 300 366 Fax 0-4-499 8383
Email lharrap@hotmail.com Website www.flybywire.co.nz

Discounts	Group
Season	Year-round
Time to allow	30 minutes
Flight time	10 minutes
Cost	$99 (includes video)
Operator's sales pitch	This is the world's only actual flight simulator! The pilot has full control of the speed and direction of the plane and the flight varies from 1 m to 55 m off the ground.

OPERATORS
SOUTH ISLAND

WHITEWATER RAFTING

Action in Marlborough

Phone 0-3-578 4531 Freephone 0800 266 266 Fax 0-3-578 4531
Email crew@actioninmarlborough.co.nz Website www.actioninmarlborough.co.nz

Discounts	NZ Outside, group
Optional extras	Action photo, T-shirt
Season	October–April (groups at other times)
Operator's sales pitch	We have run a safe rafting operation for over 20 years. We are multi-day specialists and will tailor-make trips especially for groups, including food options. We endeavour to make every trip as memorable as possible.
Other activities offered	Multi-day rafting trips on the Clarence and Buller Rivers

Gowan/Buller Rivers

River grade	3
Put-in point	Lake Rotoroa
Time to allow	Full day
Time on water	4–5 hours
Bring with you	Towel, swimsuit, footwear for river
Cost	$110 (includes transport, lunch)

Buller River

River grade	3
Put-in point	Gowanbridge
Time to allow	6–7 hours
Time on water	2–3 hours
Bring with you	Towel, swimsuit, footwear for river
Cost	$70

Buller Gorge

River grade	3
Put-in point	O'Sullivan's
Time to allow	Full day
Time on water	4–5 hours
Bring with you	Towel, swimsuit, footwear for river
Cost	$120 (includes transport, lunch)

FRENCH PASS

SWIMMING WITH DOLPHINS & SEALS

French Pass Motels & Sea Safaris

Phone 0-3-576 5204 Fax 0-3-576 5204
Email adventure@SeaSafaris.co.nz Website www.SeaSafaris.co.nz

Discounts	NZ Outside, group
Season	Year-round
Chance of seeing dolphins	50% (summer); 90% (winter)
Chance of swimming with dolphins	On demand
Guarantee	Yes (seals, fish, walks, birds, etc.)
Likely marine life seen	Bottlenose and dusky dolphins, New Zealand fur seals, king shags, penguins, petrels, gannets
Maximum number of swimmers	16 (normally 6)
Time to allow	2–4 hours
Time in water	20 minutes
Bring with you	Towel, swimsuit, warm outdoor clothing, camera, sunscreen, hat, binoculars
Cost	$78 (includes shower)
Optional extras	T-shirt, disposable camera
Operator's sales pitch	There are several reasons to come on a tour with us: few people, an island location, clear water.
Other activities offered	Nature walks, shark swimming, sport fishing, diving, sea kayaking

SWIMMING WITH SHARKS

French Pass Motels & Sea Safaris

Phone 0-3-576 5204 Fax 0-3-576 5204
Email adventure@SeaSafaris.co.nz Website www.SeaSafaris.co.nz

Discounts	NZ Outside, group
Season	December–April
Chance of swimming with sharks	98%
Guarantee	Next trip free if no sharks seen
Likely marine life seen	Blue and mako sharks, seabirds, dolphins
Maximum number of swimmers	16 (normally 6)
Time to allow	4 hours
Time in water	20 minutes
Bring with you	Towel, swimsuit, warm outdoor clothing, camera, sunscreen, hat, binoculars
Cost	$98 (includes shower)
Optional extras	T-shirt, disposable camera
Operator's sales pitch	The water in the area is exceptionally clear. All trips are recorded for a field study being submitted to the Pelagic Shark Foundation.
Other activities offered	Nature walks, dolphin/seal swimming, sport fishing, diving, sea kayaking

NELSON

TANDEM HANG GLIDING

Nelson Hang Gliding Adventures

Phone 0-3-548 9151 Mobile phone 025 751 436

Season	Year-round
Launch sites	Barnicoat Range, Takaka, Tapawera
Time to allow	2–3 hours
Flight time	15–20 minutes
Bring with you	Sunscreen, sensible shoes, warm outdoor clothing
Cost	$130
Optional extras	Action photos
Operator's sales pitch	Nelson is New Zealand's premier hang gliding region, offering mountain and sea views. We have reliable sea breezes and thermal conditions that provide excellent soaring. Flights are tailored to suit, from tranquil scenic glides through to some exciting aerobatics.
Other activities offered	Hang gliding instruction

TANDEM PARAGLIDING

Nelson Paragliding

Phone 0-3-544 1182 Mobile phone 025 463 930 Fax 0-3-544 1182

Season	Year-round
Launch site	Nelson region
Time to allow	2–3 hours
Flight time	15–20 minutes
Bring with you	Comfortable outdoor clothing, sensible shoes
Cost	$110 (includes transport, 20-minute flight)
Operator's sales pitch	Your pilot will be Stew Karstens, twice New Zealand cross-country champion. Nelson has more flying days than anywhere in New Zealand and flights have spectacular views over Nelson Bays and Abel Tasman National Park.
Other activities offered	1-day solo instruction ($150), guiding, longer instruction courses, sales

TANDEM SKYDIVING

Tandem Skydive Nelson New Zealand

Phone 0-3-545 2121 Freephone 0800 422 899 Fax 0-3-546 4242
Email tandem@skydive.co.nz Website www.nelson.co.nz/skydive/

Discounts	VIP, YHA, Kiwi Experience, Magic Bus, NZ Outside, group
Season	Year-round
Airfields	Nelson, Motueka
Time to allow	2 hours
Bring with you	Comfortable outdoor clothing, sensible shoes
Cost	$190 (9000 ft)
Optional extras	Video, action photo, T-shirt
Operator's sales pitch	With us, the tandem masters own the company. We are a small company and are particularly careful about safety matters and pay close attention to individual customers' needs.

WHITEWATER RAFTING

Rapid River Rafting Co.

Phone 0-3-545 7076 Freephone 0800 277 052 Mobile phone 025 245 9295 Fax 0-3-545 7076
Email rapidriver@xtra.co.nz Website www.rapid-river.co.nz

Discounts	NZ Outside
Optional extras	Action photo, T-shirt
Season	September–May
Operator's sales pitch	This is the one! Rapid River, the only Nelson-based rafting company, runs the longest day raft trip in New Zealand. We offer free transport, food and a full money-back guarantee. Yahoo!
Other activities offered	Multi-day rafting trips

Gowan/Buller Rivers

River grade	3 plus
Put-in point	Lake Rotoroa
Time to allow	8 hours
Time on water	4.5 hours
Bring with you	Soft-soled shoes, towel, swimsuit
Cost	$115 (includes transport, food)

Buller River

River grade	4
Put-in point	2 km south of Murchison
Time to allow	9 hours
Time on water	3.5 hours
Bring with you	Soft-soled shoes
Cost	$120 (includes transport, food)

MOTUEKA

SWIMMING WITH SEALS

Abel Tasman Seal Swim

Phone 0-3-527 8136 Freephone 0800 527 8136 Fax 0-3-527 8136

Discounts	Group, schools
Season	Year-round
Chance of seeing seals	100%
Chance of swimming with seals	98%
Guarantee	None
Likely marine life seen	New Zealand fur seals, dolphins, blue penguins, gannets, shearwaters, shags, terns
Maximum number of swimmers	12
Time to allow	3 hours
Time in water	45–60 minutes
Bring with you	Towel, swimsuit, warm outdoor clothing, camera
Cost	$78
Optional extras	Action photo, T-shirt
Operator's sales pitch	We have a guide with each swimming group. We don't go any closer than 5 m to a seal or seals. We keep the group tightly together and let the seals choose to come to us.
Other activities offered	Full water taxi service

MURCHISON

JETBOATING

Buller Experience Jet

Phone 0-3-523 9880 Mobile phone 025 220 3955 Fax 0-3-523 9880
Email pete@murchison.co.nz Website www.murchison.co.nz

Discounts	Group, family
Season	Year-round
Departures	Regular and on demand
Launch sites	Upper Buller Gorge, Riverview Motor Camp
Time to allow	40–60 minutes
Time on water	40 minutes
Cost	$60
Optional extras	Action photo, clothing
Operator's sales pitch	Our trips are simply world class – through incredible sheer rock gorges and falls, with thrills to rival any New Zealand jetboat trip. The scenery is outstanding and colour diversity amazing.
Other activities offered	Combos (rafting, kayaking, heli-rafting, heli-kayaking, heli-fishing)

WHITEWATER RAFTING

Ultimate Descents

Phone 0-3-523 9899 Freephone 0800 RIVERS (0800 748 377) Fax 0-3-523 9811
Email ultimate@rivers.co.nz Website www.rivers.co.nz

Discounts	YHA, group
Optional extras	Video, T-shirt, hat
Season	August–May
Operator's sales pitch	We are located close to New Zealand's best whitewater and offer the largest range of river trips in the country. River flows are reliable and base facilities include showers, hot tub, changing rooms and a cafe. The service is friendly and experienced. In the "Riversports" options you raft, kayak or sledge your way down the river, switching craft whenever you like.

Buller Gorge rafting

River grade	3–4
Put-in point	Dellows Bluff
Time to allow	4 hours
Time on water	2.5 hours
Bring with you	Towel, swimsuit, sunscreen
Cost	$95 (includes shower, spa, BBQ)

Buller Gorge rafting and riversports

River grade	2–4
Put-in point	Dellows Bluff
Time to allow	Full day
Time on water	4 hours
Bring with you	Towel, swimsuit, sunscreen
Cost	$125 (includes shower, spa, picnic lunch, BBQ)

West Coast heliraft extreme

River grade	4–5
Put-in point	Varies
Time to allow	Full day
Time on water	4–6 hours
Bring with you	Towel, swimsuit, sunscreen
Cost	$275 (includes helicopter, lunch)

Riversports

River grade	2–3
Put-in point	Buller Gorge swing bridge
Time to allow	3 hours
Time on water	1.5–2 hours
Bring with you	Towel, swimsuit, sunscreen
Cost	$75 (includes shower, spa)

White Water Action Rafting Tours

Phone 0-3-523 9581   Freephone 0800 100 582   Fax 0-3-523 9581

Discounts	Group, family
Optional extras	Action photo, T-shirt
Season	Year-round
Operator's sales pitch	We offer a professional, personal, colour-co-ordinated touch. We're very flexible and use top quality equipment. We will take you to the most action on the day. Inflatable kayaks are available on all tours.
Other activities offered	Multi-day trips on the Buller and its tributaries, eco tour on grade 2 river (includiing raft float, gold panning and garnet fossicking), raft fishing, canoe hire

Buller River

River grade	3 plus
Put-in point	Gowanbridge
Time to allow	4 hours
Time on water	Up to 2.5 hours
Bring with you	Towel, swimsuit, camera
Cost	$75 (includes transport ex Murchison)

Buller River

River grade	3–4
Put-in point	Buller Gorge
Time to allow	5 hours
Time on water	Up to 2.5 hours
Bring with you	Towel, swimsuit, camera
Cost	$85 (includes transport ex Murchison, BBQ lunch)

Buller River (Ariki Falls)

River grade	3–4
Put-in point	Buller Gorge
Time to allow	4 hours
Time on water	Up to 2 hours
Bring with you	Towel, swimsuit, camera
Cost	$80 (includes transport ex Murchison)

Best of the Buller

River grade	3–4
Put-in point	Murchison
Time to allow	Full day
Time on water	Up to 5 hours
Bring with you	Towel, swimsuit, camera
Cost	$110 (includes transport ex Murchison, lunch)

Karamea River

River grade	5
Put-in point	Karamea
Time to allow	Full day
Time on water	Up to 5 hours
Bring with you	Thermals, swimsuit, towel, camera
Cost	$350 (includes helicopter, lunch)

Wanganui River

River grade	4–5
Put-in point	Harihari
Time to allow	Full day
Time on water	Up to 5 hours
Bring with you	Thermals, swimsuit, towel, camera
Cost	$350 (includes helicopter, lunch)

Grey River

River grade	3–4
Put-in point	Ekimatua
Time to allow	Full day
Time on water	Up to 5 hours
Bring with you	Thermals, swimsuit, towel, camera
Cost	$175 (includes transport ex Murchison, lunch)

RIVER BUGS

Ultimate Descents

Phone 0-3-523 9899 Freephone 0800 RIVERS (0800 748 377) Fax 0-3-523 9811
Email ultimate@rivers.co.nz Website www.rivers.co.nz

Activity	River Bugs
Discounts	YHA, group
Optional extras	T-shirt, hat
Season	August–May
Operator's sales pitch	Just when you thought you'd seen it all, we bring you the world's latest whitewater craze. Experience the thrill of shooting small waterfalls and winding your way through a boulder maze, all in your own personal craft.

Buller River (upper)

River grade	2–3
Put-in point	Gowanbridge
Time to allow	4 hours
Time on water	2 hours
Bring with you	Towel, swimsuit, sunscreen
Cost	$95 (includes shower, spa, light refreshments)

ADVENTURE CAVING

Norwest Adventures

Phone 0-3-789 6686 Freephone 0800 11 66 86 Fax 0-3-789 7956
Email norwest@xtra.co.nz Website www.caverafting.com

Discounts	NZ Outside
Season	Year-round
Optional extras	Action photo, T-shirt, cameras
Operator's sales pitch	The adventure caving trip is a real caving adventure with a full range of skills learned and used – get wet and dirty. Underworld rafting has a variety of caving, glowworm and river rafting experiences in one action-filled adventure.

Adventure caving	
Time to allow	5–6 hours
Time in cave	3–4 hours
Caving elements	Squeeze, abseil, ladder, swim, slide, climb, self-caving section, formation section
Bring with you	Towel, swimsuit
Cost	$180 (includes transport, shower, camera, hot drink, map, pen)

Underworld rafting	
Time to allow	4.5–5.5 hours
Time in cave	2.5–3 hours
Caving elements	Tubes, swim, glowworms, formations and caves
Bring with you	Towel, swimsuit
Cost	$90 (includes transport, hot drink, shower, certificate, postcard, pen)

JETBOATING

Buller Adventure Tours

Phone 0-3-789 7286 Freephone 0800 697 286 Mobile phone 025 304 520 Fax 0-3-789 8104
Email adventure.tours@xtra.co.nz Website www.adventuretours.co.nz

Discounts	Kiwi Experience, Magic Bus, group, family
Season	Year-round
Departures	On demand
Launch site	Buller Adventure Tours
Time to allow	2 hours
Time on water	1.25 hours
Bring with you	Warm outdoor clothing
Cost	$55
Optional extras	T-shirt
Operator's sales pitch	Our tours are tailored to suit, and we can offer everything from passive to bruising trips. Our 8-seater high-powered jet travels at speeds of up to 90 kph in a dense green environment.
Other activities offered	Whitewater rafting, horse trekking, Argo 8 x 8 safaris

WHITEWATER RAFTING

Buller Adventure Tours

Phone 0-3-789 7286 Freephone 0800 697 286 Mobile phone 025 304 520 Fax 0-3-789 8104
Email adventure.tours@xtra.co.nz Website www.adventuretours.co.nz

Discounts	Kiwi Experience, Magic Bus, family
Season	Year-round
Operator's sales pitch	We supply personalised service, local knowledge and excellent food. For an alternative experience you can switch from raft to Funyak at will. The Buller River is the largest volume river rafted in New Zealand.
Other activities offered	Jetboat, horse trekking, Argo 8 x 8 safaris

Buller River

River grade	4
Put-in point	Earthquake
Time to allow	5 hours
Time on water	3 hours
Bring with you	Towel, swimsuit
Cost	$75 (includes transport ex Westport, BBQ)

Karamea River

River grade	5
Put-in point	Karamea
Time to allow	8–9 hours
Time on water	5–6 hours
Bring with you	Towel, swimsuit
Cost	$235 (includes helicopter, transport ex Westport or Karamea, lunch)

GREYMOUTH

ADVENTURE CAVING

Dragons Cave Rafting

Phone 0-3-768 6649 Freephone 0800 223 456
Email info@newzealandholiday.co.nz Website www.newzealandholiday.co.nz

Discounts	New Zealand 7 Wonders card
Season	Year-round
Optional extras	T-shirt, camera
Operator's sales pitch	Float a galaxy world of glowworms, slide underground waterfalls, cuddle through the love tunnel and discover enchanting limestone formations. Includes hot spa and showers. Suits all ages and abilities.
Other activities offered	4WD drive tours, whitewater tunnel rafting, multi-day trips, heli-rafting, tours

Dragons Cave

Time to allow	5 hours
Time in cave	1.5–2 hours
Caving elements	Squeeze, abseil, tubes, slide, glowworms
Bring with you	Towel, swimsuit
Cost	$95 (includes shower, light snack and drink)

Dragons Cave Rafting *(continued)*	
Harwoods Hole, Nelson	
Time to allow	Full day
Time in cave	5 hours
Caving elements	Abseil, climb
Cost	$985 (includes helicopter, food and drink, shower)

WHITEWATER RAFTING

Wild West Adventure Co.	
Phone 0-3-768 6649 Freephone 0800 223 456 Email info@newzealandholiday.co.nz Website www.newzealandholiday.co.nz	
Discounts	New Zealand 7 Wonders card
Optional extras	T-shirt, cameras
Season	Year-round
Perth River heli-rafting	
River grade	5
Put-in point	Near Whataroa
Time to allow	12 hours
Time on water	6 hours
Bring with you	Towel, swimsuit
Cost	$265 (includes helicopter, lunch)

FRANZ JOSEF

ICE CLIMBING

The Guiding Company of Franz Josef Glacier	
Phone 0-3-752 0047 Freephone 0800 800 102 Fax 0-3-752 0047 Email glacier@voyager.co.nz Website www.nzguides.com	
Discounts	VIP, YHA, Kiwi Experience, Magic Bus, group
Season	Year-round
Time to allow	8 hours
Time spent climbing	4 hours plus
Bring with you	Warm outdoor clothing, food for the day, sunscreen, camera, waterproof clothing if possible
Cost	$150 (includes transport)
Optional extras	T-shirt
Operator's sales pitch	The dynamic Franz Josef Glacier is the world's fastest advancing glacier. Climb with us, ride the ice waves and enjoy high scenery at low altitude.
Other activities offered	Full-day and half-day guided walks, heli-hikes

FOX GLACIER

ICE CLIMBING

Alpine Guides Fox Glacier

Phone 0-3-751 0825 Freephone 0800 111 600 Fax 0-3-751 0857
Email foxguides@minidata.co.nz Website www.foxguides.co.nz

Discounts	Group
Season	Year-round
Time to allow	8 hours
Time spent climbing	5 hours
Bring with you	Warm outdoor clothing, lunch, sunglasses, sunscreen, camera
Cost	$150 (includes transport)
Operator's sales pitch	We use excellent modern equipment and skilled guides. Our ice climbing sites are easily accessible.
Other activities offered	Full-day and overnight trips to climb peaks, heli-hikes, glacier walks

TANDEM SKYDIVING

Skydive New Zealand

Phone 0-3-751 0080 Freephone 0800 751 0080 Mobile phone 025 359 123 Fax 0-3-768 4777
Email skydivenz@yahoo.com

Discounts	Kiwi Experience, Magic Bus, group, family
Season	Year-round
Airfields	Fox Glacier, Franz Josef
Time to allow	1–2 hours
Bring with you	Comfortable outdoor clothing, sensible shoes
Cost	$255 (12,000 ft)
Optional extras	Video, action photo, T-shirt
Operator's sales pitch	This is the most spectacular skydive in New Zealand. Fly right beside Mt Cook, looking down on glaciers and mountains on one side, and sea on the other. We have 3 tandem masters with 20 years' experience.
Other activities offered	Accelerated freefall

SWIMMING WITH DOLPHINS

Dolphin Encounter

Phone 0-3-319 6777 Freephone 0800 SEE DOLPHINS (0800 733 365) Fax 0-3-319 6534
Email info@dolphin.co.nz Website www.dolphin.co.nz

Discounts	Group, family
Season	Year-round
Chance of seeing dolphins	99%
Chance of swimming with dolphins	99%
Guarantee	None
Likely marine life seen	Dusky and occasionally common and Hector's dolphins, orcas, pilot whales
Maximum number of swimmers	13 swimmers plus viewers
Time to allow	3 hours
Time in water	10–45 minutes
Bring with you	Towel, swimsuit, warm outdoor clothing, camera
Cost	$95 (includes shower)
Operator's sales pitch	Kaikoura is one of the best places in the world to encounter and swim with wild dolphins.
Other activities offered	Albatross encounters

New Zealand Sea Adventures

Phone 0-3-319 6622 Freephone 0800 SCUBA DIVE (0800 728 223) Fax 0-3-319 6868
Email nzsa.wildlife@xtra.co.nz Website www.scubadive.co.nz

Discounts	VIP, YHA, Kiwi Experience, Magic Bus, NZ Outside, group, family
Season	Year-round
Chance of seeing dolphins	99%
Chance of swimming with dolphins	98%
Guarantee	Full refund if no dolphins found
Likely marine life seen	Dusky dolphins, New Zealand fur seals, seabirds
Maximum number of swimmers	20
Time to allow	3.5 hours
Time in water	20–30 minutes
Bring with you	Towel, swimsuit
Cost	$85 (includes hot drinks, biscuits)
Optional extras	T-shirt
Operator's sales pitch	All staff are well trained. Trips are not back-to-back, which allows for more time on the water when conditions are good.
Other activities offered	Seal swimming, diving, dive training

SWIMMING WITH SEALS

Graeme's Seal Swimming Adventure

Phone 0-3-319 6182 Mobile phone 025 886 235 Fax 0-3-319 6186
Email sealswim@clear.net.nz Website www.kaikoura.co.nz/sealswim/index.htm

Discounts	NZ Outside, group, family
Season	November–April
Chance of seeing seals	98%
Chance of swimming with seals	95%
Guarantee	50% discount if seals do not swim with us
Likely marine life seen	New Zealand fur seals
Maximum number of swimmers	10
Time to allow	2.5 hours
Time in water	1–1.25 hours
Bring with you	Towel, swimsuit
Cost	$40 (includes shower)
Optional extras	Action photo, T-shirt
Operator's sales pitch	We don't use boats as they disturb the seals' habitat. Each group has a guide with a large float that young children, disabled and older people can hold on to.
Other activities offered	Ski trips to Mt Lyford Alpine Resort in winter

New Zealand Sea Adventures

Phone 0-3-319 6622 Freephone 0800 SCUBA DIVE (0800 728 223) Fax 0-3-319 6868
Email nzsa.wildlife@xtra.co.nz Website www.scubadive.co.nz

Discounts	VIP, YHA, Kiwi Experience, Magic Bus, NZ Outside, group, family
Season	October–April
Chance of seeing seals	100%
Chance of swimming with seals	98%
Guarantee	Viewing-only price if seals not found in water
Likely marine life seen	New Zealand fur seals, seabirds
Maximum number of swimmers	13
Time to allow	3 hours
Time in water	1 hour
Bring with you	Towel, swimsuit
Cost	$45 (includes hot drinks, biscuits, shower)
Optional extras	T-shirt
Operator's sales pitch	Our trips are boat-based so sites can be alternated. You get a better experience and we can keep clear of the areas where seals have a lot of human contact.
Other activities offered	Dolphin swimming, diving, dive training

SWIMMING WITH SHARKS

Shark Dive Kaikoura

Phone 0-3-319 6888 Freephone 0800 2 C JAWS (0800 225 297) Fax 0-3-319 5713
Email suzannekay@xtra.co.nz Website www.kaikoura.co.nz/shark

Discounts	Group
Season	December–April
Chance of swimming with sharks	90%
Guarantee	None
Likely marine life seen	Blue and mako sharks
Maximum number of swimmers	10
Time to allow	5 hours
Time in water	Varies
Bring with you	Towel, swimsuit, hat, jacket, sunscreen, dive cert if any
Cost	$110 (includes shower)
Optional extras	Action photo, T-shirt
Operator's sales pitch	We take small groups and have friendly, helpful staff.

CHEVIOT

JETBOATING

Turf to Surf

Freephone 0800 279 479 Fax 0-3-319 8921 Email turf.to.surf@xtra.co.nz

Season	Year-round
Departures	On demand
Launch site	Turf to Surf base
Time to allow	1.5 hours
Time on water	40 minutes
Bring with you	Warm outdoor clothing
Cost	$50
Operator's sales pitch	We offer a jetboat ride in an area of New Zealand that is only accessible by jetboat. We are the only operators in this area of the Waiau River.
Other activities offered	Fishing, 4WD safari, farm stays

HANMER SPRINGS

BUNGY JUMPING

Thrillseekers Adventure Centre Thrillseekers Canyon, Main Road, Hanmer Springs

Phone 0-3-315 7046 Fax 0-3-315 7057
Email an.cameron.adventure@xtra.co.nz Website www.thrillseeker.co.nz

Season	Year-round
Time to allow	15 minutes
Bungy height	35 m
Water entry available	Yes
Cost	$95
Optional extras	Action photo, T-shirt
Operator's sales pitch	Enjoy a brilliant freefall and float under a historic bridge. One site offers it all: bungy, jetboating, river rafting, shop, good coffee.
Other activities offered	Jetboat, self-drive jetboats, whitewater rafting, team building

GUIDED ADVENTURES

Rainbow Adventures

Phone 0-3-315 7401 Mobile phone 025 578 578 Fax 0-3-315 7401
Email rainbowadventures@xtra.co.nz Website www.rainbowadventures.co.nz

Discounts	VIP, group, family
Operator's sales pitch	We offer excellent service and years of experience. We are proud to be pioneers in adventure tourism – we are New Zealand's original Funyak and canyoning company.
Other activities offered	Longer Funyak and rafting trips, paragliding holidays, leadership and team-building courses

Canyoning

Location	Hanmer Springs
Activity	Walk, jump, slide and explore a small canyon in a family adventure. Relive your childhood and enjoy the fun and freedom of waterfalls and water holes.
Season	September–May
Time to allow	2 hours
Bring with you	Good shoes
Cost	$42

Whitewater rafting

Location	Hurunui River
Activity	Experience the ultimate in beauty and action on a grade 3–4 river.
Season	September–May
Time to allow	Full day
Cost	$98 (includes transport, lunch)

Rainbow Adventures *(continued)*	
Funyaks	
Location	Boyle River, Waiau River
Activity	Paddle 1- or 2-person inflatable, self-bailing canoes through grade 2–3 rapids in a mountain setting.
Season	September–May
Time to allow	Half day
Cost	$60
Tandem paragliding	
Location	Mt Isobel, Wallace Peak
Activity	Take our Mt Isobel flight for double fun: fly by helicopter to the top of Mt Isobel and glide like an eagle 3300 ft back to the Hanmer township. For a shorter flight take the Wallace Peak option.
Season	Year-round
Time to allow	3 hours
Bring with you	Sensible shoes
Cost	$135 (includes transport)

JETBOATING

Thrillseekers Adventure Centre

Phone 0-3-315 7046 Fax 0-3-315 7057
Email an.cameron.adventure@xtra.co.nz Website www.thrillseeker.co.nz

Season	Year-round
Departures	Hourly and on demand
Launch site	Thrillseekers Canyon
Time to allow	20 minutes
Time on water	20 minutes
Bring with you	Sunglasses, warm outdoor clothing
Cost	$45
Optional extras	Video, action photo, T-shirt
Operator's sales pitch	Our jetboat trip is New Zealand's best, guaranteed! We can go faster, further, take you on a scenic, adventure or whitewater trip – the choice is yours. Bring your camera and snap a bungy jumper or a raft floating by, or just relax and enjoy the scenery.
Other activities offered	Longer jetboat trips, bungy, whitewater rafting

SELF-DRIVE JETBOATING

Thrillseekers Adventure Centre

Phone 0-3-315 7046 Fax 0-3-315 7057
Email an.cameron.adventure@xtra.co.nz Website www.thrillseeker.co.nz

Season	Year-round
Departures	On demand
Launch site	Thrillseekers Canyon
Time to allow	20 minutes
Time on water	10 minutes
Cost	$25
Optional extras	Action photo
Operator's sales pitch	We offer a specially designed mini jetboat that you drive around a specially designed course. If you're over 15 years old just have a go – put yourself in the driving seat!
Other activities offered	Bungy, whitewater rafting

RIVER RAFTING

Thrillseekers Adventure Centre

Phone 0-3-315 7046 Fax 0-3-315 7057
Email an.cameron.adventure@xtra.co.nz Website www.thrillseeker.co.nz

Optional extras	Action photo, T-shirt
Season	Year-round
Operator's sales pitch	We do it better! From a few hours to a few days: raft the spectacular Waiau, Hurunui, Boyle and Clarence Rivers.
Other activities offered	Multi-day rafting trips, jetboat, bungy, scenic rafting

Waiau River

River grade	3
Put-in point	Thrillseekers Canyon
Time to allow	Half day
Time on water	1.5–2.5 hours
Cost	$65

Waiau River (top canyon)

River grade	3 plus
Put-in point	Wilderness area
Time to allow	Half day
Time on water	3 hours
Cost	$140 (includes 4 x 4 transport)

Boyle River

River grade	3 plus
Time to allow	Half day
Time on water	1 hour
Cost	$90

SPRINGFIELD

JETBOATING

Waimak Alpine Jet

Phone 0-3-318 4881 Freephone 0800 26 36 26 Fax 0-3-318 4883
Email waimak.alpine.jet@xtra.co.nz Website www.waimakalpinejet.co.nz

Discounts	Group, family
Season	Year-round
Departures	Regular and on demand
Launch site	Springfield
Time to allow	4 hours
Time on water	30 minutes
Bring with you	Warm outdoor clothing, sunglasses, camera
Cost	From $45
Optional extras	Action photo
Operator's sales pitch	Waimak Alpine Jet offers the best in scenery and excitement. The awe-inspiring Waimakariri Canyon is regarded as one of the most spectacular river canyons in the world. Absolutely incredible! Longer trips also available, as are transfers from Christchurch.

CASTLE HILL

GUIDED ADVENTURES

Irie Tours

Phone 0-3-318 7669 Fax 0-3-318 7559

Discounts	All rates negotiable
Operator's sales pitch	We are New Zealand's only alpine canyoning operation, and we offer a wide range of other activities with the emphasis on fun and good times for all.

Alpine canyoning

Location	Arthur's Pass National Park
Activity	Take an hour-long walk up a well-formed track to the first abseil station at the top of the canyon. Abseil 35 m to the canyon floor, then travel the length of the canyon, plunging over another 6 waterfalls and finishing, if desired, with a 3-pitch 115-m waterfall abseil to the carpark.
Season	Summer
Time to allow	Full day
Bring with you	Warm outdoor clothing, lunch, sunscreen
Cost	$135

Abseiling

Location	Castle Hill rocks
Activity	Get full tuition in abseiling. Enjoy a number of abseils from the low angle starter through to the big one.
Season	Year-round
Time to allow	2–3 hours
Bring with you	Warm clothes, camera, sunscreen, runners
Cost	$65 (includes hot drinks)

Rock climbing

Location	Castle Hill rocks
Activity	Get tuition and guiding in rock climbing.
Season	Year-round
Time to allow	Half day
Bring with you	Warm clothes, food
Cost	$125 (includes hot drinks)

Adventure caving

Location	Cave stream
Activity	Ascend the underground river running through one of New Zealand's youngest limestone caves.
Season	Summer
Time to allow	2–3 hours
Bring with you	Warm clothes, change of clothes
Cost	$65 (includes hot drinks)

CHRISTCHURCH

AEROBATIC FLIGHTS

Barnstormers

Phone 0-3-343 5542 Mobile phone 025 321 135 Fax 0-3-348 4366 Email skydive@xtra.co.nz

Season	Year-round
Aeroplane	Pitts Special S2-A
Range of Gs	Minus 3 to plus 6
Time to allow	1 hour
Flight time	20 minutes
Cost	$195
Optional extras	Action photo
Operator's sales pitch	The Pitts Special was specially designed and built for aerobatics. It is a legend in its own right and can offer the ultimate in aerobatic flying. A biplane designed in the late 1940s, it is still a leader today in the world of aerobatics.
Other activities offered	Skydiving

GUIDED ADVENTURES

Peak Experience

Phone 0-3-384 3262 Fax 0-3-384 3262 Email peakx@clear.net.nz

Operator's sales pitch	Our guides are skilled and qualified, and we offer personal attention to clients.

Rock climbing

Location	Port Hills
Activity	Try your hand at rock climbing on a top rope.
Season	Year-round
Time to allow	8 hours
Bring with you	Warm outdoor clothing, food
Cost	$300 for up to 4 people

HOT AIR BALLOONING

Up Up and Away

Phone 0-3-358 9859 Mobile phone 025 325 611 Fax 0-3-358 9829
Email info@ballooning.co.nz Website www.ballooning.co.nz

Season	Year-round
Time to allow	3–4 hours
Flight time	1 hour
Bring with you	Warm outdoor clothing, camera
Cost	$200 (includes transport, certificate)
Optional extras	Action photos
Operator's sales pitch	There is no other place in the world where it is possible to fly from the centre of the city in view of the ocean towards snow-capped mountains.

TANDEM PARAGLIDING

Cloud Nine Paragliding

Phone 0-3-385 4739 Mobile phone 025 382 060 Fax 0-3-385 8038

Season	Year-round
Launch site	Port Hills
Time to allow	2 hours
Flight time	10–20 minutes
Bring with you	Comfortable outdoor clothing, sensible shoes
Cost	$110 (includes transport ex city, T-shirt)
Optional extras	Action photo, T-shirt
Operator's sales pitch	Ours is a family business, very friendly and experienced. We offer the best flight possible in the conditions. Free T-shirt!

Nimbus Paragliding

Phone 0-3-326 7922 Mobile phone 025 324 874
Email nimbus.pg@xtra.co.nz Website www.newsoftland.co.nz/nimbusparagliding

Season	Year-round
Launch site	Taylors Mistake (Sumner), Port Hills, Christchurch gondola
Time to allow	1 hour
Flight time	10 minutes
Bring with you	Comfortable outdoor clothing, sensible shoes
Cost	$95
Optional extras	Action photo, T-shirt, cap
Operator's sales pitch	Awesome! Longer, 20-minute flights are also available.
Other activities offered	1-day solo instruction ($165)

Phoenix Paragliding

Phone 0-3-326 7634 Mobile phone 025 332 794 Fax 0-3-326 7634
Email phoenix@paragliding.co.nz Website www.paragliding.co.nz

Season	Year-round
Launch site	Port Hills
Time to allow	1.5 hours
Flight time	15–20 minutes
Bring with you	Comfortable outdoor clothing, sensible shoes
Cost	$120
Optional extras	Video, action photo, T-shirt
Operator's sales pitch	Using the safest, top-performing equipment we fly our passengers higher and longer from our exclusive Port Hills sites, with excellent views. Our pilots are highly experienced, allowing more dramatic manoeuvres.
Other activities offered	1-day solo instruction ($165), guided tours throughout New Zealand, sales, safety training courses

TANDEM SKYDIVING

Christchurch Parachute School

Phone 0-3-343 5542 Mobile phone 025 321 135 Fax 0-3-348 5542
Email skydive@xtra.co.nz Website www.skydiving.co.nz

Discounts	Kiwi Experience, Magic Bus
Season	Year-round
Airfield	Wigram
Time to allow	2 hours
Bring with you	Comfortable outdoor clothing, sensible shoes
Cost	$245 (Wigram DZ, includes transport)
Optional extras	Video, action photo, T-shirt
Operator's sales pitch	We're very conveniently located 15 minutes from central Christchurch.
Other activities offered	Accelerated freefall

AKAROA

SWIMMING WITH DOLPHINS

Dolphin Experience Akaroa

Phone 0-3-304 7726 Freephone 0508 DOLPHINS (0508 365 744) Fax 0-3-304 7726
Email dolphin.experience@clear.net.nz

Discounts	YHA, group, family (direct bookings only)
Season	Year-round
Chance of seeing dolphins	99%
Chance of swimming with dolphins	90%
Guarantee	Viewing-only price ($35) if we don't swim
Likely marine life seen	Hector's dolphins, blue penguins, New Zealand fur seals, seabirds
Maximum number of swimmers	12
Time to allow	3 hours
Time in water	80 minutes (varies seasonally)
Bring with you	Swimsuit, camera
Cost	$75 (includes hot refreshments, shower)
Optional extras	T-shirt, cap, postcards
Operator's sales pitch	Swim or spend time with the rare Hector's dolphin. See the grace and beauty of these small dolphins in their natural environment.
Other activities offered	Outer bay tours, cruises, harbour tours

METHVEN

HOT AIR BALLOONING

Aoraki Balloon Safaris

Phone 0-3-302 8172 Freephone 0800 CLOUD 7 (0800 256 837) Fax 0-3-302 8162
Email calm@voyager.co.nz Website www.nzballooning.com

Discounts	NZ Outside, group, family, New Zealand 7 Wonders, Air NZ Holiday Rewards, Explore NZ, Hertz Rentals, National Car Rentals
Season	Year-round
Time to allow	4 hours
Flight time	1 hour approx.
Bring with you	Warm outdoor clothing, hat, video, camera, binoculars
Cost	$255 (includes transport, champagne breakfast, certificate)
Operator's sales pitch	Methven is well recognised as New Zealand's finest ballooning location, with pristine views of Mt Cook and a 300-km panorama of the Canterbury Plains (by Mt Hutt). It's a tranquil, romantic, enthralling air adventure.

TANDEM SKYDIVING

Christchurch Parachute School

Phone 0-3-343 5542 Mobile phone 025 321 135 Fax 0-3-348 5542
Email skydive@xtra.co.nz Website www.skydiving.co.nz

Discounts	Kiwi Experience, Magic Bus
Season	Ski season
Airfield	Pudding Hill
Time to allow	2 hours
Bring with you	Comfortable outdoor clothing, sensible shoes
Cost	$245 (includes transport)
Optional extras	Video, action photo, T-shirt
Operator's sales pitch	We have some of the most capable instructors and staff from around New Zealand. Our facilities, equipment and experience are hard to beat.
Other activities offered	Accelerated freefall

ASHBURTON

TANDEM SKYDIVING

Adventure Skydives Aviation

Phone 0-3-307 0495 Freephone 0800 666 228 Mobile phone 025 224 6529 Fax 0-3-307 0497
Email dgrice@xtra.co.nz

Discounts	Group
Season	Year-round
Airfields	Ashburton, Twizel/Mt Cook
Time to allow	2 hours
Bring with you	Comfortable outdoor clothing, sensible shoes
Cost	$215 (9000 ft)
Optional extras	Video, action photo, T-shirt, air-to-air still shots
Operator's sales pitch	We offer a friendly country atmosphere, great views of the Pacific coastline, Southern Alps and Canterbury Plains, and ultra-modern facilities in a self-contained hangar.
Other activities offered	Accelerated freefall ($350), aerobatic joyrides

GERALDINE

WHITEWATER RAFTING

Rangitata Rafts

Phone 0-3-696 3735 Freephone 0800 251 251 Mobile phone 025 332 449 Fax 0-3-696 3534
Email rangitatarafts@xtra.co.nz Website www.rafts.co.nz

Discounts	Kiwi Experience, Magic Bus, group
Optional extras	Action photo, T-shirt
Season	October–May
Operator's sales pitch	The Rangitata is the closest commercially rafted grade 5 river to Christchurch, and it is consistently grade 5 at all water levels. We're located off the beaten track and offer personalised service.

Rangitata Gorge	
River grade	5
Put-in point	Peel Forest
Time to allow	Full day
Time on water	3 hours
Bring with you	Towel, swimsuit
Cost	$115 (includes transport ex Christchurch, lunch, shower, BBQ)

TWIZEL

GUIDED ADVENTURES

Southern Alps Guiding

Phone 0-3-435 0890 Mobile phone 025 342 277 Fax 0-3-326 7518
Email charles@outside.nz.com Website www.mtcook.com

Discounts	NZ Outside

Rock climbing and kayaking

Location	Mt Cook
Activity	Spend half a day rock climbing and abseiling, then half a day glacier sea kayaking. If you prefer, do just one of the activities.
Season	Year-round
Time to allow	Full day
Cost	$165

WANAKA

AEROBATIC FLIGHTS

Biplane Adventures

Phone 0-3-443 1000 Freephone 0508 WARBIRDS (0508 927 247) Mobile phone 025 362 909
Fax 0-3-443 1006 Email biplane@skyshow.co.nz Website www.biplane-adventures.co.nz

Discounts	YHA, Kiwi Experience, Magic Bus
Season	Year-round
Aeroplanes	Pitts Special, Tiger Moth, T6-Harvard, P-51 Mustang
Range of Gs	Minus 3 to plus 6
Time to allow	30 minutes–1 hour
Flight time	15 minutes
Cost	$170 (Pitts Special or Tiger Moth flight, includes certificate)
Optional extras	T-shirt
Operator's sales pitch	Our aircraft have dual controls so passengers can fly them. They are beautifully restored and maintained classics.
Other activities offered	Joyrides in classic and vintage aircraft

JETBOATING

Clutha River Jet

Phone 0-3-443 7495 Fax 0-3-443 1323

Discounts	Group, family
Season	Year-round
Departures	Hourly and on demand
Launch site	The wharf
Time to allow	1 hour
Time on water	1 hour
Bring with you	Warm outdoor clothing
Cost	$60
Operator's sales pitch	Relax and enjoy a 15-minute jaunt across the lake with unsurpassed views and an informative commentary before entering the mighty Clutha River. Skim over rocks and sandbars, power through rapids and giant pressure waves.
Other activities offered	Cruises, guided fishing trips, lake kayak hire, mountain bikes

TANDEM PARAGLIDING

Lucky Montana's Flying Circus

Freephone 0800 CIRCUS (0800 247 287) Fax 0-3-443 1681

Season	December–April
Launch site	Wanaka
Time to allow	30 minutes
Flight time	15–20 minutes
Bring with you	Comfortable outdoor clothing, sensible shoes
Cost	$130
Optional extras	Action photos, clothing
Operator's sales pitch	Ours is the only tow-launched paraglider in New Zealand. Don't walk or be driven up – be towed to 3000 ft behind a boat on the lake. We specialise in aerobatics and taking up people with disabilities and the elderly.
Other activities offered	Half-day solo instruction ($150), guiding

TANDEM SKYDIVING

Tandem Skydive Wanaka

Phone 0-3-443 7207 Mobile phone 025 796 877
Email skydive@skyshow.co.nz Website www.skydivenz.com

Season	Year-round
Airfield	Wanaka
Time to allow	1.5 hours
Bring with you	Comfortable outdoor clothing, sensible shoes
Cost	$225 (9000 ft)
Optional extras	Video, action photo, clothing
Operator's sales pitch	Wanaka, with its incredible views of Mt Cook, Mt Aspiring and 4 sparkling lakes, is a breathtaking place to skydive. We place great importance on customer safety and satisfaction and have a 100% safety record.

WHITEWATER KAYAKING

Alpine River Guides

Phone 0-3-443 9023 Mobile phone 025-382 475 Fax 0-3-443 9553
Email paddle@alpinekayaks.co.nz Website www.alpinekayaks.co.nz

Discounts	YHA, NZ Outside, group
Optional extras	T-shirt
Season	September–April
Operator's sales pitch	We can offer instruction on a variety of kayaks, including sit-on-top kayaks. The scenery in the Wanaka region, gateway to Mt Aspiring National Park, is beautiful: take the chance to learn about the river environment, fauna and flora, and local history.
Other activities offered	Harder trips for experienced paddlers

Hawea River (dam controlled)

River grade	2 plus
Put-in point	Lake Hawea
Time to allow	8–9 hours
Time on water	5–6 hours
Bring with you	Towel, swimsuit, camera
Cost	$120 (includes lunch, afternoon tea)

Upper Clutha River

River grade	2
Put-in point	Lake Wanaka outlet
Time to allow	8–9 hours
Time on water	5–6 hours
Bring with you	Towel, swimsuit, camera
Cost	$120 (includes lunch, afternoon tea)

Matukituki River

River grade	1–2
Put-in point	Raspberry Creek
Time to allow	10 hours
Time on water	4–5 hours
Bring with you	Towel, swimsuit, camera
Cost	$120 (includes transport, lunch, afternoon tea)

WHITEWATER SLEDGING

Frogz Have More Fun

Phone 0-3-443 9130 Freephone 0800 338 737 Mobile phone 025 338 737 Fax 0-3-443 8244
Email frogz_nz@yahoo.com Website www.frogz.co.nz

Discounts	YHA, Kiwi Experience, Magic Bus, NZ Outside, group
Optional extras	T-shirt
Season	November–April
Operator's sales pitch	Popular in Europe, whitewater sledging is a competitive river sport. The sledges are purpose-designed for rivers and you are in control.

Frogz Have More Fun *(continued)*

Clutha River

River grade	1–2
Put-in point	Wanaka
Time to allow	4–5 hours
Time on water	2 hours
Bring with you	Towel, swimsuit
Cost	$75 (includes transport, refreshments)

Hawea River (dam controlled)

River grade	2–3
Put-in point	Wanaka
Time to allow	4 hours
Time on water	1.5–2 hours
Bring with you	Towel, swimsuit
Cost	$85 (includes transport, refreshments)

Kawarau River

River grade	2–4
Put-in point	Wanaka
Time to allow	4–5 hours
Time on water	1.5 hours
Bring with you	Towel, swimsuit
Cost	$95 (includes transport, refreshments)

QUEENSTOWN

AEROBATIC FLIGHTS

Actionflite Aerobatics

Phone 0-3-442 9708 (master agent) Freephone 0800 360 264 (Actionflite)
Mobile phone 025 360 264 (pilot) Fax 0-3-442 7038
Email actionflite@actionflite.co.nz Website www.actionflite.co.nz

Discounts	VIP, YHA, Kiwi Experience, NZ Outside, group
Season	Year-round
Aeroplane	Pitts Special
Range of Gs	Minus 3 to plus 6
Allow	1 hour
Flight time	15–20 minutes
Cost	$195 (includes certificate)
Optional extras	Video, action photo, T-shirt
Operator's sales pitch	Flights go to a minimum of 5000 ft above spectacular Queenstown, with outstanding lake and mountain views. The thrill factor begins with a gentle tingle and can build to a full-scale, 5-star buzz. Aircraft undergo full inspection by engineers every 50 flight hours.
Other activities offered	Tiger Moth scenic flights

BUNGY JUMPING

AJ Hackett Bungy

Phone 0-3-442 7100 Freephone 0800 BUNGY JUMP (0800 286 495) Fax 0-3-442 7121
Email bungyjump@ajhackett.co.nz Website www.ajhackett.com

Season	Year-round
Time to allow	Varies
Bungy height	43 m (Kawarau), 47 m (The Ledge), 134 m (Nevis)
Water entry available	Yes (Kawarau only)
Bring with you	Covered-in footwear (Nevis only), warm outdoor clothing
Cost	$125 (Kawarau), $99 (Ledge), $174 (Nevis) – includes transport and T-shirt
Optional extras	Video, action photo, clothing
Operator's sales pitch	The Kawarau bungy was the world's first full-time bungy operation. The Ledge is the ultimate urban bungy experience with night jumps in winter and tandem jumps available. At the Nevis Highwire Bungy you jump 134 m from the world's only purpose-built bungy gondola.
Other activities offered	All 3 bungy jumps for $229, combos (bungy, jetboat, raft, helicopter, river surfing, luge)

Pipeline Bungy

Phone 0-3-442 5455 Freephone 0800 BUNGY 1 (0800 286 491) Mobile phone 025 201 8155
Fax 0-3-442 4029 Email bungy@pipeline.co.nz Website www.bungy.co.nz

Discounts	YHA, Kiwi Experience, Magic Bus, group
Season	Year-round
Time to allow	3 hours
Bungy height	102 m
Water entry available	No
Bring with you	Warm outdoor clothing, comfortable footwear, light snack
Cost	$135 (includes transport, certificate)
Optional extras	Video, action photo, cap
Operator's sales pitch	We have excellent facilities and fantastic views in a historic gold-mining canyon.
Other activities offered	Flying fox, jetboat, 4WD trips, helicopter, combos available

CANYONING

Twelve Mile Delta Canyoning

Freephone 0800 2 CANYON (0800 222 696) Mobile phone 025 507 677, 025 392 746
Fax 0-3-442 3315 Email canyoning@xiimile.co.nz Website www.xiimile.co.nz

Discounts	YHA, Kiwi Experience, Magic Bus
Season	1 October–late April
Canyon	Twelve Mile Creek
Time to allow	3.5 hours
Time in water	2 hours
Bring with you	Towel, swimsuit, drinking water
Cost	$95 (includes transport, BBQ sausage)
Optional extras	T-shirt
Operator's sales pitch	Our canyoning experience is conducted on the Ancient Moonlight Seabed with rock that has oyster shells, seashells, as well as beautiful, stunning surroundings.

FLY BY WIRE

Fly by Wire

Phone 0-3-442 2116 Mobile phone 025 300 474 Fax 0-3-442 2116
Email lharrap@hotmail.com Website www.flybywire.co.nz

Discounts	Group
Season	Year-round
Time to allow	2–3 hours
Flight time	10 minutes
Cost	$129 (includes transport)
Optional extras	Video, clothing
Operator's sales pitch	This is the world's fastest land-based adventure ride! The pilot has full control of the speed and direction of the plane and the flight varies from 3 m to 100 m off the ground.

FLYING FOX

Skippers Flying Fox

Phone 0-3-442 5455 Freephone 0800 286 491 Fax 0-3-442 4029
Email sales@flyingfox.co.nz Website www.grandcanyon.co.nz

Discounts	YHA, Kiwi Experience, Magic Bus
Season	Year-round
Time to allow	3 hours
Ride time	1 minute
Ride length	200 m
Maximum height	102 m
Bring with you	Camera, snack, jacket, sunglasses
Cost	$79 (includes transport, including commentary)
Optional extras	Hot drinks, soft drinks
Operator's sales pitch	Skippers Flying Fox is in a unique historic location. It is high, long and dramatic with breathtaking views of Skippers Canyon, but is still a gentle ride.
Other activities offered	Bungy, jetboat, 4WD historical trip, combos available

GUIDED ADVENTURES

Independent Mountain Guides

Phone 0-3-442 3381 Mobile phone 025 352 005 Fax 0-3-442 3381 Email imguides@xtra.co.nz

Operator's sales pitch	Our qualified guides are all "unique" personalities. Excursions are tailor-made with clients receiving a huge adventure. A great margin of safety is delivered.
Other activities offered	Mountaineering, ski touring, snowboard touring

Rock climbing	
Location	Sites around Queenstown
Activity	Learn to climb, abseil, place protection, rig anchors, possibly lead
Season	September–May
Time to allow	6 hours
Bring with you	Food and drink, sports clothing
Cost	$110 (includes transport)

Independent Mountain Guides (continued)

Ice climbing

Location	Remarkables
Activity	Learn to climb, use crampons and ice axes, place ice gear, abseil.
Season	June–September
Time to allow	8 hours
Bring with you	Food, drink, warm outdoor clothing
Cost	$250 (includes transport)

Mountain Works

Phone 0-3-442 7329 Mobile phone 025 220 5950 Fax 0-3-442 7329
Email mtnworks@queenstown.co.nz Website www.mountainworks.co.nz

Discounts	Group
Operator's sales pitch	We provide professional mountain guides and quality equipment for fun, safe mountain adventures. We enjoy sharing our love and knowledge of the mountains and guiding you to explore places you have only dreamed about.
Other activities offered	Abseiling, ropes/confidence course, alpine climbing

Rock climbing

Location	Sites around Queenstown
Activity	Learn to set up equipment and climb safely – including learning about ropes, knots and belaying. Tackle several climbs at your level.
Season	Year-round
Time to allow	7 hours
Bring with you	Sensible shoes, lunch
Cost	$99

Mountaineering

Location	Remarkables
Activity	Make the walk to the ridge – use crampons and ice axes in winter, use rock gear in summer – and make the summit.
Season	Year-round
Time to allow	8–9 hours
Bring with you	Lunch
Cost	$195

HOT AIR BALLOONING

Sunrise Balloons

Phone 0-3-441 8248 Freephone 0800 HOT AIR (0800 468 247) Fax 0-3-442 5387
Email balloons@queenstown.co.nz

Discounts	YHA
Season	Year-round
Time to allow	3.5 hours
Flight time	1 hour
Bring with you	Warm outdoor clothing, sensible shoes, maybe a hat
Cost	$295 (includes transport, champagne breakfast)
Optional extras	Action photo, handpainted champagne glasses
Operator's sales pitch	Great scenery, great food!
Other activities offered	Charter flights

JETBOATING

Kawarau Jet

Phone 0-3-442 6142 Freephone 0800 KAWARAU (0800 529 272) Fax 0-3-442 2239
Email jetboat@queenstown.co.nz Website www.kjet.co.nz

Discounts	VIP, NZ Outside, group, family
Season	Year-round
Departures	Hourly
Launch site	Main town pier
Time to allow	1.25 hours
Time on water	1 hour
Bring with you	Warm outdoor clothing in winter
Cost	$65 (includes admission to Queenstown Underwater World)
Optional extras	Action photo, clothing
Operator's sales pitch	Ours is the longest jetboat trip in Queenstown, through beautiful scenery you can't see unless you're in a jetboat. We'll take you on 2 rivers – the Shotover and the Kawarau, and give you more thrills and spins.
Other activities offered	Combos (rafting, helicopter, bungy, river surfing)

Shotover Jet

Phone 0-3-442 8570 Freephone 0800 SHOTOVER (0800 746 868) Fax 0-3-442 7467
Email reservations@shotoverjet.co.nz Website www.shotoverjet.com

Season	Year-round
Departures	Every 15 minutes
Launch site	Arthurs Point
Cost	$75 (includes transport ex Queenstown)
Optional extras	Action photos, clothing
Operator's sales pitch	We are the only jetboat operator in the world-famous Shotover River canyons, and have the world's most exciting jetboat ride.

Skippers Canyon Jet

Phone 0-3-442 5455 Freephone 0800 286 491 Fax 0-3-442 4029
Email admin@grandcanyon.co.nz Website www.grandcanyon.co.nz

Season	Year-round
Departures	Regular
Launch site	Skippers Canyon
Time to allow	3 hours
Time on water	40 minutes
Bring with you	Camera, food, jacket, sunglasses, hat in winter
Cost	$79 (includes transport, hot drinks and biscuits)
Optional extras	Video, action photo, T-shirt
Operator's sales pitch	Our company culture makes us special. We have professional personnel and purpose-built boats with the world's first fully integrated computerised motor/driver safety system. Our unique environment gives all the right ingredients for high adventure.
Other activities offered	Bungy, flying fox, 4WD historical trip, combos available

Twin Rivers Jet

Phone 0-3-442 3257 Freephone 0800 107 747 Fax 0-3-442 2829
Email twinjet@queenstown.co.nz Website www.twinriversjet.co.nz

Discounts	YHA, NZ Outside, group
Season	Year-round
Departures	Hourly
Launch site	Main town pier
Time to allow	1.25 hours
Time on water	1 hour
Bring with you	Warm outdoor clothing in winter, sunglasses, sunscreen
Cost	$59
Optional extras	Action photo, clothing
Operator's sales pitch	We have a well-priced 45-km round trip on 3 waterways: Lake Wakatipu, Kawarau River and Shotover River (most of the trip is on the Shotover). The boat departs from the very centre of Queenstown. Get ready for brilliant thrills and scenery.
Other activities offered	Combos (rafting, helicopter, gondola, horse riding)

LUGE

Skyline Luge Brecon Street, Queenstown

Phone 0-3-441 0101 Fax 0-3-442 6391
Email gondola@skyline.co.nz Website www.skyline.co.nz

Season	Year-round
Time to allow	1 hour
Bring with you	Warm outdoor clothing in winter
Cost	$22 (includes 5 luge rides, gondola)
Optional extras	Action photo, T-shirt
Operator's sales pitch	The luge is a unique New Zealand concept, an activity where you ride at your level with no pressure to perform. The rider is in control – you create your own fun and thrills.
Other activities offered	Cafe, walking tracks

TANDEM HANG GLIDING

Antigravity Hang Gliding

Freephone 0800 HANG GLIDE (0800 426 445) Email antigravity@xtra.co.nz

Season	Nearly year-round (some time off in winter)
Launch sites	Queenstown Hill, Coronet Peak, Crown Range
Time to allow	1.5–2 hours
Flight time	7–30 minutes (depends on presence of lifting air)
Bring with you	Warm outdoor clothing, sensible shoes
Cost	$145 (includes transport)
Optional extras	Action photos, T-shirt
Operator's sales pitch	We can go higher and usually stay up longer than our competitors. We have world-ranked competition pilots who aim to give passengers the best flight possible. We use the best equipment. Passengers aren't kept waiting while someone else flies.
Other activities offered	Heli-hang gliding from higher launch sites, flights from the top of the Coronet Peak chairlift in winter, longer flights

Antigravity Hang Gliding *(continued)*

Phone 0-3-442 6311 Mobile phone 025 331 741 Fax 0-3-442 7706 Email skytrek@xtra.co.nz

Season	Year-round
Launch sites	Coronet Peak, Remarkables Range, Crown Terrace
Time to allow	2–3 hours
Flight time	10–20 minutes
Bring with you	Warm outdoor clothing, sensible shoes
Cost	$145 (includes transport)
Optional extras	Action photos, T-shirt
Operator's sales pitch	We have the best selection of launch sites so there's more chance to get airborne. We were the first tandem hang gliding company in New Zealand and have recorded more than 18,000 tandem flights.

TANDEM PARAGLIDING

In Queenstown the main paragliding site is off Bobs Peak at the top of the Skyline gondola, where 15 tandem pilots operate from a taxi stand above the main building. There's no need to book - just show up and take your turn.

High Adventure Paragliding

Freephone 0508 HIGH ADVENTURE (0508 44 44 23)

Season	Year-round
Launch site	Coronet Peak
Time to allow	1.5 hours
Flight time	15–20 minutes
Bring with you	Comfortable outdoor clothing, sensible shoes
Cost	$130 (includes transport)
Optional extras	Action photos, T-shirt
Operator's sales pitch	A 20-minute scenic drive takes us to our 3500-ft launch site. We'll soon be soaring in this spectacular alpine setting of lakes and mountains. A 3-km cross-country flight takes us to the landing zone near historic Arrowtown.
Other activities offered	Longer flights, heli-tandems

Max Air Tandem Parapente

Phone 0-3-442 7770 Mobile phone 025 324 147

Season	Year-round
Launch sites	Skyline Queenstown, Coronet Peak
Time to allow	1.25 hours
Flight time	10–15 minutes
Bring with you	Comfortable outdoor clothing, sensible shoes
Cost	$130 (includes gondola)
Optional extras	Action photos, T-shirt
Operator's sales pitch	Fly over Queenstown with New Zealand's longest established paragliding business.
Other activities offered	Longer instruction courses, heli-tandem

Queenstown Tandem Parapentes

Freephone 0800 4 PARAGLIDE (0800 472 724) Mobile phone 025 332 517
Email brundel@es.co.nz Website www.zqn.co.nz/parapente

Season	Year-round
Launch sites	Skyline Queenstown, Coronet Peak
Time to allow	1 hour
Flight time	8–10 minutes
Bring with you	Comfortable outdoor clothing, sensible shoes
Cost	$160 (includes action photos, 2 gondola rides)
Optional extras	T-shirt, cap
Operator's sales pitch	Our state-of-the-art tandem paragliders fly 2000 ft over the spectacular Wakatipu basin.
Other activities offered	Heli-tandem from Bowen Peak

Renegade Tandem Parapentes

Phone 0-3-442 9584 Mobile phone 025 332 541 Fax 0-3-442 5693

Season	Year-round
Launch sites	Skyline Queenstown, Coronet Peak
Time to allow	1 hour
Flight time	10–20 minutes
Bring with you	Comfortable outdoor clothing, sensible shoes
Cost	$130 (includes gondola)
Optional extras	Action photos, T-shirt
Operator's sales pitch	Renegade was the first company in New Zealand to teach paragliding, the world's fastest-growing aviation sport.
Other activities offered	Heli-tandem

TANDEM SKYDIVING

Skydive Tandem (The Ultimate Jump)

Phone 0-3-442 5867 Mobile phone 021 325 961 Fax 0-3-442 8869
Email jump@skydivetandem.co.nz Website www.skydivetandem.co.nz

Season	Year-round
Airfield	Queenstown
Time to allow	3 hours
Bring with you	Comfortable outdoor clothing, sensible shoes
Cost	$245 (9000 ft – includes transport, certificate)
Optional extras	Freefall video and photos, clothing
Operator's sales pitch	Queenstown's scenery is unsurpassed. Customer service, professionalism and safety are hallmarks of this small company. We have carried more than 20,000 passengers over 9 years with an unblemished safety record.

WHITEWATER RAFTING

Challenge Rafting

Phone **0-3-442 7318** Freephone **0800 4 ADVENTURE** (**0800 423 836**) Fax **0-3-441 8563**
Email **challenge@raft.co.nz** Website **www.raft.co.nz**

Discounts	YHA
Optional extras	Action photo, T-shirt
Season	Year-round
Operator's sales pitch	Our guides are friendly and professional. We offer hot showers, sauna and refreshments at the Rafters Lodge.
Other activities offered	Combos including options of helicopter flight, jetboat, bungy and gondola

Shotover River

River grade	3–4
Put-in point	Deep Creek
Time to allow	5 hours
Time on water	1.5 hours
Bring with you	Towel, swimsuit
Cost	$119 (includes transport, sauna, shower, refreshments)

Kawarau River

River grade	2–3
Put-in point	Chard Farm
Time to allow	5 hours
Time on water	1 hour
Bring with you	Towel, swimsuit
Cost	$109 (includes transport, sauna, shower, refreshments)

Extreme Green Rafting

Phone **0-3-442 8517** Mobile phone **025 356 946** Fax **0-3-442 8510**
Email **extremeg@queenstown.co.nz** Website **www.extremegreenrafting.com**

Discounts	YHA, Kiwi Experience, Magic Bus, group, family
Optional extras	Action photo, T-shirt
Season	Year-round
Operator's sales pitch	We are a small owner/operator company specialising in personal service with an emphasis on safety. We offer the best value for money.

Shotover River

River grade	3–4
Time to allow	4.5 hours
Time on water	1.5–2 hours
Bring with you	Towel, swimsuit
Cost	$109 (includes transport, BBQ snack, shower)

Kawarau River

River grade	3–4
Time to allow	4 hours
Time on water	1 hour
Bring with you	Towel, swimsuit
Cost	$89 (includes transport, refreshments)

Queenstown Rafting

Phone 0-3-442 9792 Freephone **0800 RAFTING** (0800 723 846) Fax 0-3-442 4609
Email qtn.raft@xtra.co.nz Website www.rafting.co.nz

Discounts	YHA, Magic Bus
Optional extras	Action photo
Season	Year-round
Operator's sales pitch	We are New Zealand's largest operator, specialising in the historic Shotover River.
Other activities offered	Combos: Triple Challenge (rafting, jetboat, helicopter), Twin Challenge (rafting, jetboat), Crazy Kiwi (rafting, helicopter, jetboat, bungy jump)

Shotover River

River grade	3–4
Put-in point	Deep Creek
Time to allow	4.5 hours
Time on water	2 hours
Bring with you	Towel, swimsuit
Cost	$119 (includes transport, sauna, shower, hot drinks)

Kawarau River

River grade	2–3
Put-in point	Chard Farm
Time to allow	4 hours
Time on water	1 hour
Bring with you	Towel, swimsuit
Cost	$100 (includes transport, sauna, shower, hot drinks)

WHITEWATER SLEDGING & RIVER BOARDING

Frogz Have More Fun

Phone 0-3-443 9130 Freephone **0800 338 738** Fax 0-3-443 8244
Email frogz_nz@yahoo.com Website www.frogz.co.nz

Discounts	YHA, Kiwi Experience, Magic Bus, NZ Outside, group
Optional extras	T-shirt
Season	November–April
Operator's sales pitch	Popular in Europe, whitewater sledging is a competitive river sport. The sledges are purpose-designed for rivers and you are in control.

Kawarau River

River grade	2–4
Time to allow	4–5 hours
Time on water	1.5 hours
Bring with you	Towel, swimsuit
Cost	$98 (includes transport, refreshments)

Mad Dog River Boarding

Phone 0-3-442 9708 Mobile phone 025 440 089 Fax 0-3-442 3310
Email maddog@queenstown.co.nz

Discounts	YHA, Kiwi Experience, Magic Bus, NZ Outside, group, family
Optional extras	Action photo, T-shirt, hat, cap
Season	September–May
Operator's sales pitch	A jetski with a rescue sledge gives us full access to the entire section of the river we run, improving safety considerably.

Kawarau River (Roaring Meg)

River grade	3–4
Put-in point	Roaring Meg
Time to allow	4.5 hours
Time on water	1.25 hours
Bring with you	Towel, swimsuit
Cost	$99 (includes transport)

Kawarau River

River grade	3–4
Put-in point	Gibbston–Chard Farm
Time to allow	4 hours
Time on water	1 hour
Bring with you	Towel, swimsuit
Cost	$99 (includes transport)

Serious Fun River Surfing

Phone 0-3-442 5262 Freephone 0800 737 468 Mobile phone 021 122 262 Fax 0-3-442 5265
Email sfun@voyager.co.nz Website www.riversurfing.com

Discounts	VIP, YHA, Magic Bus, NZ Outside, group, family, locals, film crews
Optional extras	Action photo, T-shirt
Season	September–May
Operator's sales pitch	We invented the sport of river boarding a decade ago and are now international, with another operation on the Zambezi in Africa. We have small, personalised groups of 10 for maximum enjoyment and safety.

Kawarau River (Roaring Meg)

River grade	2–4
Put-in point	Roaring Meg
Time to allow	4 hours
Time on water	1–2 hours
Bring with you	Towel, swimsuit
Cost	$109 (includes T-shirt, beer)

Kawarau River (Dog Leg)

River grade	2–4
Time to allow	3–4 hours
Time on water	1–2 hours
Bring with you	Towel, swimsuit
Cost	$109 (includes transport, T-shirt, beer)

COMBOS

If you're planning to do some serious adventuring in the "Adventure capital of the world", you can save money and time by booking your extreme trips as part of a combo instead of individually.

If your adrenal glands are up to it, Queenstown Combos can organise a monster day of action for you. Helicopter ride, bungy jump, whitewater rafting, jetboating, Skippers Road, Skyline Gondola? You choose what you want to do. Queenstown Rafting also has combo deals with helicopter, jetboat and bungy operators, while the Skippers Grand Slam gives you the Skippers Road, jetboating, a flying fox ride and a bungy jump.

DUNEDIN

TANDEM SKYDIVING

Parachute Experience	
Phone 0-3-489 4113 Mobile phone 025 370 371 Fax 0-3-216 9669 Email DAVE-JO.D@zfree.co.nz	
Discounts	Group, family
Season	Year-round
Airfield	Taieri
Time to allow	1–2 hours
Bring with you	Comfortable outdoor clothing, sensible shoes
Cost	$230 (9000 ft)
Optional extras	Video, action photos (book ahead), transport available
Operator's sales pitch	See excellent views of the Otago harbour and coastline when you skydive. On clear days you can see both Mt Cook and Mt Aspiring.
Other activities offered	Accelerated freefall $255, static line courses $180

INDEX